PLAYS FROM
HISPANIC TALES

Plays from Hispanic Tales

One-act, royalty-free dramatizations for young people, from Hispanic stories and folktales

By

BARBARA WINTHER

Publishers   PLAYS, INC.   *Boston*

Y
812
W

Library of Congress Cataloging-in-Publication Data

Winther, Barbara.
  Plays from Hispanic tales / by Barbara Winther.
      p.   cm.
  Contents: El caballito of seven colors—The ghost of el castillo
—The great Hurricane—Brother Rabbit sells corn—Pedro de
Urdemalas—Latino trio—The talking burro—A gift for
Pachacuti Inca—The deer dance—The sleeping mountains—
Macona, the honest warrior.
  ISBN 0-8238-0307-4 (alk. paper)
  1. Children's plays, American. 2. Folklore—Latin American—
Juvenile drama. 3. Tales—Latin American   Adaptations.
4. Folklore—Spain—Juvenile drama. 5. Tales—Spain—Adapta-
tions.
  [1. Folklore—Latin America—Drama. 2. Folklore—Spain—
Drama.
3. Plays.] I. Title.
PS3573.I558P58   1998
812'.04089282—dc21   97-51973
                                                      CIP
                                                      AC

Manufactured in Canada

To "the kids"—Dave, Mike and Cheryl

CONTENTS

ACKNOWLEDGMENTS

Many thanks to the following: Elizabeth Santillan, Language Consultant; Dr. Guadalupe M. Friaz, Lecturer, Chicano Studies Program, Department of American Ethnic Studies, University of Washington; Mimi Fellores, teacher, Bainbridge Island Public Schools; Dr. Jack Bunn, former resident in and student of Central and South American countries; and Grant A. Winther, my husband, who went with me everywhere, listened to everything, and made helpful comments on it all.

INTRODUCTION

Described through cave paintings or told orally, folktales are the oldest art form. From earliest times, the stories people handed down from one generation to the next defined who they were and what they wanted future generations to know—the passing of the torch, an illumination of a culture.

My aim in writing this book of plays based on Hispanic folktales is to encourage the study of the many facets of Hispanic culture. I hope those who act in and produce one of these plays will examine its background first. What is the environment like? How do these characters live—their food, clothing, shelter? What do they need? What do they desire? What are their fears, their beliefs, their concepts of right and wrong? What do they think is serious or funny? How have things changed? What comparisons and contrasts can be made between this particular folktale and how we live today? Between how *señoritas* and *señor*s were then, and how they are now?

Pick up the torch, shine it around, uncover more about Hispanic folklore and its reflection on Hispanic life.

—BARBARA WINTHER

El Caballito of Seven Colors

The tale of a magical horse of seven colors was brought to the Americas from Spain. Versions appear on islands in the Caribbean, in Mexico, in New Mexico and Texas—wherever the Spanish colonized. Throughout Europe and Russia, similar tales are told of a magical creature who aids poor peasants.

In certain versions, the horse of seven colors helps Juan bring back a gold ring from the bottom of the sea in order to win the woman he loves. In some tales it is intimated that "The City" is on the Gulf of Mexico, but in other tales "The City" is further north. Often, one of the guests is to bring back the beautifully feathered quetzal bird from deep in the rain forest. Juan rides the horse of seven colors in many versions, and sometimes Juan del Dedo (John Finger) is Juan's name, and he is described as a tiny boy as big as a finger. The field where the horse eats is occasionally wheat instead of corn; sometimes the *alcalde* is a king; in certain versions the older brothers come to a bad end.

I mention these variations, and there are many more, to illustrate that there is seldom one version of a folktale. The story takes on the environment where it is told, includes what the teller thinks will interest the listener, and involves creativity in presentation. In a similar way, to adapt this and other folktales to the stage, I found it necessary to make modifications. However, the essence of the story, the meaning of it, is always retained.

El Caballito of Seven Colors

Characters

The Diego Family
  PADRE, (*father*), *a farmer*
  MADRE, (*mother*)
  CARLOS, *oldest son*
  LUIS, *middle son*
  JUAN, *youngest son*
EL CABALLITO, (*the little horse*)
EL ALCALDE, (*the mayor*)
LISETA, *his daughter*
TWO SERVANTS

SCENE 1

BEFORE RISE: *Sound of rooster crowing is heard.* SER-
VANTS *enter before curtain;* 1ST SERVANT *holds up
sign that reads:* AN EARLY SUMMER MORNING IN 1820,
and 2ND SERVANT *holds up sign that reads:* IN A CORN-
FIELD IN NEW MEXICO. *Then they exit. Curtain opens.*
SETTING: *Dark backdrop curtain. Cardboard cutouts of ten
cornstalks, one knocked down, two eaten-clean cobs near it.*
AT RISE: *Stage is empty.* PADRE *enters right, sees trampled
stalk and rushes to inspect it.*

PADRE (*Falling to knees; lamenting loudly*): ¡Ay! ¡Ay! ¡Ay!
  (MADRE *rushes on right, followed by* CARLOS *and*

LUIS, *both sleepy,* and JUAN, *who always carries a guitar.*)

MADRE (*Concerned*): What is wrong, husband?

PADRE: Last night, someone entered our cornfield, trampled this stalk (*Points at flattened stalk*), and devoured these ears of corn. (*Picks up cobs, then tosses them behind stalks*)

MADRE (*In dismay*): ¡Madre Dios! I hope we won't lose any more corn.

PADRE (*Rising*): So do I, but I fear this could happen again.

MADRE (*Alarmed*): If we lose our corn, we will starve. (*Spreads arms wide*) How can I feed five people for a year on one sack of *frijoles* and a string of hot peppers?

PADRE (*Groaning*): It could be the end of the Diego family.

CARLOS (*Puffing out chest*): Don't worry. Give me a rope, and I, Carlos, your eldest and strongest son, will guard the cornfield tonight. I shall catch the thief and tie him up.

MADRE: But, Carlos, you are such a sleepyhead. I doubt if you can stay awake all night.

CARLOS (*Boastfully*): Of course I can, Mama. (*Swaggers over to his father*) Papa, give me a rope, and I will save our corn. (*Blackout.* PADRE, MADRE, LUIS, *and* JUAN *exit right.* CARLOS, *wrapped in serape, rope in hand, sits center, head buried in arms on hunched knees as if asleep. Lights up dim; moonlight on* CARLOS, *who snores. Sound of crickets is heard.* EL CABALLITO *enters left, stamps on a cornstalk with hooves, and pantomimes eating corn to sounds of crunching.*)

EL CABALLITO (*To audience*): That lazy boy (*Points hoof at* CARLOS) didn't guard his family's field. (*Whinnies in disgust and gallops off left. Rooster crows off right. Lights up full.* PADRE *enters right, sees new trampled stalk, and rushes to inspect it.*)

PADRE (*Falling to knees; upset*): ¡Ay! ¡Ay! ¡Ay! (CARLOS *wakes up, stretches, and yawns.* MADRE *rushes on right, followed by sleepy* LUIS *and* JUAN.)

MADRE (*Hopefully*): Carlos, did you catch the thief?

CARLOS: Thief? (*Looks at rope and remembers*) Oh, the thief. Well, he didn't come last night.

PADRE (*Angrily*): He *did* come, while you slept, and now more corn has been eaten.

CARLOS (*Surveying stalk*): Hm-m-m, well, well. More corn gone. What a shame! (LUIS *crosses to* CARLOS.)

LUIS: Give me that rope, Carlos. (*Grabs it*) You may be the eldest, but I, Luis, the middle son of this Diego family, have more sense. (*Crosses center*) Tonight *I* will guard the corn field.

CARLOS: You? Why, you can't even catch a (*Indicates a bug scurrying on ground*)—a *cucaracha*.

LUIS (*Upset*): I've caught more cockroaches than you.

CARLOS: Well, you can't catch a thief. (*Crosses arms*) Hm-m-m. It looks as if all our corn might be stolen. I could end up hungry if I stay around here. I'm leaving.

MADRE (*Tearfully*): Leaving? Carlos, where will you go?

CARLOS: To the city, to seek fame and fortune.

PADRE (*Upset*): What about us?

CARLOS: I care only about myself. *Adiós.* (*Exits left.* MADRE *bursts into tears and hides face in apron;* PADRE *comforts her.*)

LUIS: Don't worry. Tonight *I'll* catch the corn thief.

MADRE: But, Luis, you, too, are a sleepyhead. I doubt if you can stay awake all night.

LUIS: Of course, I can. (*Boastfully*) Papa, give me the rope and a hard chair to help me stay awake, and I'll save our corn. (*Blackout.* PADRE, MADRE, *and* JUAN *exit right.* LUIS, *wrapped in serape, rope in hand, sits center on chair, head drooped as if asleep. Lights up dim; spot on* LUIS, *who snores. Sound of crickets as before.* EL CABALLITO *enters left, tramples another stalk, and pantomimes eating corn to crunching sounds.*)

EL CABALLITO (*To audience*): Another lazy boy. (*Points hoof at* LUIS *and shakes head*) Can't anybody in the family guard this corn field? (*Whinnies as before, exits left, galloping. Rooster crows off right. Lights up full.* PADRE *enters right, sees newly trampled stalk, and rushes to inspect it.*)

PADRE (*Kneeling by corn; lamenting loudly*): ¡Ay! ¡Ay! ¡Ay! (LUIS *jumps up, blinks awake, sees trampled stalk, and hits head with dismay.* MADRE *rushes on right, followed by* JUAN.)

MADRE (*Hopefully*): Luis, did you catch the thief?

LUIS (*Ashamed*): No, I fell asleep.

PADRE (*Rising, angrily*): And now more corn has been eaten. (*Hurls sombrero to ground*) This thief will steal our entire crop. The Diego family will starve.

MADRE: What shall we do?

LUIS (*Backing away left*): I don't want to end up hungry. I'm going to follow Carlos to the city. If I find fame and fortune, I'll (*Pauses to get idea*)—I'll send you some money. *Adiós.* (*Runs off left.* MADRE *bursts into tears and hides face in apron;* PADRE *comforts her.*)

JUAN (*Crossing center*): Don't worry. Tonight I, Juan, the youngest son of this Diego family, will guard the cornfield. I'll sit on the hard chair, the rope on the ground beside me. To keep awake, I'll play my guitar.

PADRE (*Picking up sombrero, dusting it*): Juan, you've always helped me in the corn field. Perhaps you can succeed where your lazy, boastful brothers cannot. (*Blackout.* PADRE *and* MADRE *exit right.* JUAN *sits on chair, rope on ground, guitar ready to play. Lights up dim; sound of crickets; spot on* JUAN, *who strums guitar and sings a love song in Spanish. After song,* EL CABALLITO *whinnies off left.* JUAN *quickly sets guitar down, picks up rope, and hides behind chair.* EL CABALLITO *enters left and starts to trample another stalk.* JUAN *sneaks up, loops rope over horse's head, holding on to rope end. Crickets cease.* EL CABALLITO *whinnies, kicks, and struggles, not seeing* JUAN.)

EL CABALLITO: Who threw this rope around my neck?

JUAN (*Shouting*): I, Juan Diego. (EL CABALLITO *turns and sees* JUAN, *then gives up, sinking to ground.*)

EL CABALLITO: All right, Juan Diego, you've caught me.

JUAN: *Sí,* little thief. Finally! Why do you keep eating our corn?

EL CABALLITO: I eat in many fields, not just yours. For a long time I've hoped someone would catch me.

JUAN: Why?

EL CABALLITO: Because I would prefer to pay in service for what I eat. You see, I'm not a common thief.

JUAN: You don't appear to be. Your coat is magnificently colored. What is your name?

EL CABALLITO: *El Caballito* of Seven Colors. I am a magic horse. If you let me go, I promise never to come to this field again. What is more, I will grant you three wishes. To call me, just say these words:

> *El Caballito* of Seven Colors,
> I, Juan Diego, set you free;
> *El Caballito* of Seven Colors,
> Mind your vow and come to me.

JUAN: I'll trust you, little horse. (*Removes rope from neck*) You are free to go.

EL CABALLITO: *Gracias,* Juan Diego. Now you can safely go to sleep. We'll meet again three more times. (*Exits left, trotting*)

JUAN (*Examining stalks*): So much corn gone. I don't

think my family will have enough to eat. (*Looks left, raises index finger as he gets idea, calls*)

> El Caballito of Seven Colors,
> I, Juan Diego, set you free;
> El Caballito of Seven Colors,
> Mind your vow and come to me.

EL CABALLITO (*Reentering left*): Already you request your first wish?

JUAN: *Sí.* Restore the stalks you trampled, and bring back the corn you stole. I want to be sure my family has enough food.

EL CABALLITO: It's a rare person who will use a wish to help others. (*Sets up flattened cornstalks*) There. The corn field is whole again.

JUAN: *Gracias,* little horse.

EL CABALLITO: *De nada.* You have two more wishes. (*Whinnies and exits left, galloping. JUAN returns to chair, wraps serape around himself, and droops head as if asleep. Sound of crickets until rooster crows off right. Lights up full. PADRE enters right, sees JUAN asleep, and gasps, but then sees cornfield restored and is elated.*)

PADRE (*Shouting*): ¡Qué sorpresa! What a surprise! (*JUAN leaps up, startled. PADRE waves hat excitedly.*)

JUAN: *I caught the thief, Papa!* (MADRE *runs on.*)

PADRE (*Throwing up arms ecstatically*): How can this be? Juan, what happened last night?

JUAN: I stayed awake by singing and playing my guitar and thinking about a beautiful *señorita,* whose face I often see in my dreams. Near dawn I caught the thief—a magic little horse of seven colors. It promised never to come back, so I let it go. Then, it restored the corn field. (PADRE *and* MADRE *happily embrace* JUAN.)

PADRE: You have saved the Diego family.

MADRE: If only Carlos and Luis could see how much you've helped us, maybe they wouldn't be so lazy.

JUAN: I'll go to the city to find my brothers. Surely now they'll want to come home.

MADRE (*Starting off*): I'll pack some *tortillas* and *frijoles* for your journey. (*Exits*)

PADRE: And you must take my big *sombrero* (*Hands it to* JUAN) to protect you from the sun. (*Curtain*)

* * * * *

SCENE 2

BEFORE RISE: SERVANTS *enter center before curtain and set up balcony.* 1ST SERVANT *holds up sign that reads* MANY DAYS LATER, *and* 2ND SERVANT *holds up sign that reads* THE CITY, *then they exit.* LISETA *enters center curtain and stands on balcony reading a book.* JUAN *enters left, sees* LISETA, *and stares at her dumbfoundedly.*

JUAN (*To audience, gesturing*): There is the lady I see in my dreams. (*He sinks to one knee, strums his guitar, and sings a love song in Spanish.* LISETA, *enthralled, peers over her book and bats eyes at him flirtatiously.*)

LISETA (*After song*): A charming song, *señor.*

JUAN (*Rising*): I dedicate it to the beautiful *señorita.* (*Gestures to her, removes sombrero, bows.* LISETA *takes flower from hair and tosses it to him.* JUAN *tucks flower in sash.*)

LISETA: Will you return tomorrow and serenade me again?

JUAN: I will come back forever and ever to serenade you, lovely lady of my dreams. (*Replaces sombrero on head.* EL ALCALDE *enters center onto balcony.*)

EL ALCALDE (*Sternly*): Liseta, come inside. You must not speak to strangers.

LISETA: But Papa, he is such a handsome man, and he sings so romantically.

EL ALCALDE (*Grasping* LISETA*'s arm*): All the more reason for you not to speak to him. Go to your room. (*Exits center, following* LISETA. CARLOS *and* LUIS *enter right, surprised to see* JUAN.)

CARLOS: What are you doing here?

JUAN (*Extending arms happily*): Ah, Carlos and Luis, I came to bring you home.

CARLOS: We don't want to go home.

JUAN: But I caught the thief.

CARLOS *and* LUIS (*In unison, shocked*): You did?

JUAN: *Sí.* It was a magic horse, and it restored the corn field and promised never to eat there again.

LUIS: Where is this magic horse?

JUAN: I let it go.

LUIS: What? You *bobo,* you could've sold that horse for a great sum of money.

JUAN: But I wanted to set it free.

CARLOS: You really are a *bobo.* (EL ALCALDE *reenters center.*)

EL ALCALDE (*To* JUAN): Young man, I demand to know your name.

JUAN (*Removing sombrero and bowing head*): Juan Diego, at your service, *señor.*

EL ALCALDE: I am *El Alcalde* of this town.

JUAN: The town is lucky to have such a fine mayor.

EL ALCALDE: I do not seek your flattery, Juan Diego. You serenaded my daughter, Liseta. What are your intentions?

JUAN: I have none, for I am not a rich and famous man. If I were, I would beg your permission to marry Liseta. In my dreams I have often seen her face.

EL ALCALDE: How strange! My daughter claims you are in *her* dreams. This is most upsetting. Now she weeps in her room, afraid I will not let her see you again.

JUAN (*Eagerly*): Is there any way I can prove myself worthy to be her husband?

EL ALCALDE: I doubt it, but I shall consider that matter.

CARLOS (*Aside to* LUIS): I've seen this *señorita* called Liseta. She is indeed beautiful. I'd like a chance to win her hand.

LUIS (*Aside to* CARLOS): You'd have to get rid of Juan first.

CARLOS (*Still aside*): I know how to do that. Just listen to me. (*Crosses to* EL ALCALDE *and bows*) *Por favor, El Alcalde,* my name is Carlos Diego, and this (*Indicates*) is my brother Luis. (LUIS *bows.*) Our younger brother here (*Indicates* JUAN) has told us many times that to win the lady of his dreams he would undertake the most difficult task at the farthest reaches of the world. Isn't that right, Luis? (*Pokes* LUIS)

LUIS: What? Oh, *sí, sí.*

JUAN (*Perplexed*): Did I say that? (*Shrugs*) No matter. I would do anything to win Liseta.

EL ALCALDE (*Stroking chin*): A difficult quest—an excellent solution! (*Gets idea, claps hands, then cries*) I have it! Juan Diego, kneel before me. (JUAN *kneels.* EL ALCALDE *places hand on* JUAN's *head.*) To prove you worthy of my daughter's hand, I send you off to find a puppet I lost fifty years ago when my family rode north from Mexico City.

JUAN (*Gulping in disbelief*): A puppet lost fifty years ago?

EL ALCALDE: *Sí.* It has the face of an old man.

JUAN (*Rising, worried about task*): Where did you lose this puppet?

EL ALCALDE: Some place in the desert.

JUAN: Any idea where?

EL ALCALDE: If I knew where, I would have found it

long ago and given it to Liseta. I think she would like
my little puppet.

JUAN (*Replacing sombrero, speaking bravely*): Then, somehow, some way, I shall find it.

CARLOS (*Aside to* LUIS): That ought to get rid of Juan.
(EL ALCALDE *exits center,* CARLOS *and* LUIS *exit
right,* JUAN *exits left.* SERVANTS *remove balcony, then
reenter.* 1ST SERVANT *holds up sign that reads* MANY
DAYS LATER, *and* 2ND SERVANT *holds up sign that reads*
IN THE MIDDLE OF THE DESERT; *they exit. Curtain opens.*)

* * *

SETTING: *Large cardboard cutout of cactus is up center.
Upstage of cactus is old-man puppet.*

AT RISE: SERVANTS *hide behind cactus.* 1ST SERVANT
holds rattle, and 2ND SERVANT *has snake hand puppet.*
JUAN *enters left, wearily, and looks about, searching
around the edges of curtain and below stage.*

JUAN: This desert is huge. I need help. No way can I
find the puppet by myself. (*Calls*)
>   *El Caballito* of Seven Colors,
>   I, Juan Diego, set you free;
>   *El Caballito* of Seven Colors,
>   Mind your vow and come to me.

(EL CABALLITO *neighs off right then enters right,
trotting.*)

EL CABALLITO: Are you ready for your second
wish, Juan?

JUAN (*Nodding*): Sí. Fifty years ago, *El Alcalde* lost a
puppet with the face of an old man. He wants to give
it to his daughter, Liseta. I need you to find it for me.

EL CABALLITO: An easy wish to grant. The puppet
is behind that cactus. (*Points with hoof at cactus.* JUAN,
elated, starts toward it. EL CABALLITO *shouts.*) Wait!
Coiled around the puppet is *La Serpiente Cascabel.*

(JUAN *freezes.*) And, since I hate rattlesnakes, I'm afraid you are on your own to deal with this problem. *Adiós* and good luck. (*Gallops off right*)

JUAN (*Calling nervously*): *La Serpiente Cascabel,* are you behind the cactus? (1ST SERVANT *shakes rattle.* JUAN *nods to audience, gulps.*) The rattlesnake is indeed behind the cactus. Somehow, I must distract it. (*Looks at guitar and gets idea*) I know. I'll play my guitar and sing a lullaby. Maybe the rattlesnake will fall asleep. (*Strums guitar and sings a lullaby in Spanish.* 2ND SERVANT's *hand, wearing a snake puppet, creeps around side of cactus, slithers up to top, eventually falls asleep.* JUAN *stops playing, tiptoes over, grabs old-man puppet, and rushes off right, yelling.*) I found the puppet. (*Snake puppet "wakes up" suddenly, hisses after* JUAN; 2ND SERVANT *shakes rattle furiously. Quick curtain*)

* * * * *

SCENE 3

BEFORE RISE: SERVANTS *enter before curtain and set up balcony; they hold up same two signs used at start of Scene 2; then exit.* LISETA *enters center curtain and stands on balcony, fanning herself, shading eyes, and gazing left.* CARLOS, *flowers in hand, enters right and kneels to right of balcony and clears throat, trying in vain to get* LISETA's *attention.* LUIS *enters right, frowns at* CARLOS, *and shakes his head.* LISETA *sees* JUAN *in the distance.*

LISETA (*Excitedly calling over shoulder*): Papa, Papa. It's Juan. He's coming back. I see him. (EL ALCALDE *enters center onto balcony.* LISETA *points left.*)

EL ALCALDE (*Shading eyes, peering left*): Sí, and he's carrying something besides his guitar. (JUAN *enters left with puppet.*) Do my eyes deceive me? (JUAN *removes sombrero and bows to* EL ALCALDE, *holds up puppet. Happily*) My eyes do not deceive me. Juan Diego has found my long-lost puppet!

LISETA: Juan is a hero!

CARLOS (*Leaping to feet in astonishment*): Juan found the puppet? (*To* LUIS) How can this be possible?

LUIS (*To* CARLOS, *in disbelief*): It appears that Juan has more sense than we thought. He caught the thief and saved our family's cornfield; he found the puppet missing for 50 years; and now he's won the mayor's beautiful daughter!

CARLOS (*To* LUIS): Perhaps he is not such a *bobo* after all.

LUIS (*Nodding*): Sí. We are the *bobos*. (LISETA *comes down from balcony and joins hands with* JUAN.)

EL ALCALDE (*Holding up arms, proclaiming loudly*): Come into our patio, friends. We shall celebrate the coming marriage of my daughter Liseta to Juan Diego. (LISETA, JUAN, *and* EL ALCALDE *exit through center curtain.* CARLOS *and* LUIS *exit right.* SERVANTS *remove balcony, then exit. Curtain opens.*)

* * *

SETTING: *Same backdrop curtain.*

AT RISE: 1ST SERVANT *and* CARLOS *perform Mexican Hat Dance.* LISETA, JUAN, 2ND SERVANT, LUIS, *and* EL ALCALDE *stand around, clapping to music. When dance is over, all applaud and cheer.*

LISETA: I am so happy, Juan.

JUAN: I am the happiest man alive. If my *madre* and *padre* were here, my happiness would be complete. (*Remembers; raises an arm excitedly*) Wait! I can make a wish. (*Calls*)

El Caballito of Seven Colors
I, Juan Diego, set you free;
El Caballito of Seven Colors,
Mind your vow and come to me.

(EL CABALLITO *neighs off left, then enters, trotting, stopping before* JUAN. *Others gasp in wonder.* CARLOS *and* LUIS, *astonished, come forward to inspect horse.*)

EL CABALLITO: *Buenos días,* Juan Diego. I am ready to grant you your third wish.

JUAN (*Nodding*): Little magic horse, bring my mama and papa here to be honored guests at my marriage.

EL CABALLITO: Remember, Juan, this is your final wish. You can ask for power or money or good health for the rest of your life.

JUAN: I have no desire for power; I shall make my own money; as for good health—I will try my best to keep it. What is most important to me is for my family to share in my time of joy.

EL CABALLITO: Hm-m-m, all three of your wishes have been aimed at helping others.

JUAN: *Sí,* but by helping others, I have helped myself.

EL CABALLITO: I am happy to grant your wish. *Adiós,* Juan Diego. It's been a pleasure knowing you. (*Exits left, galloping*)

JUAN (*Calling after horse*): *Adiós, El Caballito, y gracias.* (*Sound of whinny off left, then* MADRE *and* PADRE *enter left.* JUAN *runs to embrace them.* CARLOS *and* LUIS *back away ashamed.*) Mama and Papa, this is *El Alcalde.* (EL ALCALDE *shakes hands with* PADRE, *who bows head;* MADRE *curtsies as* EL ALCALDE *bows to her.*) This is *El Alcalde's* daughter, Liseta, my bride-to-be. (LISETA *curtsies elegantly. Thrilled,* MADRE *curtsies, and* PADRE *bows.*) And here (*Indicates*) are your sons, Carlos and Luis. (CARLOS *and* LUIS *draw back.* PADRE *and* MADRE *give them stern looks.* JUAN, *mischievously*) I have often heard my brothers say they were sorry they ran away from home. (MADRE *and* PADRE *smile.*) Isn't that so, Carlos and Luis?

CARLOS (*Earnestly*): Mama and Papa, we are truly sorry.

LUIS: Will you take us back home again?

MADRE *and* PADRE (*Embracing them, in unison*): Of course we will.

ALL (*Sighing and rolling eyes*): Ah!

EL ALCALDE (*Proclaiming*): Continue the family celebration. Tomorrow is the wedding, and after that, a *fiesta* for all of the city to enjoy. (*All cheer and start to dance and sing. Curtain slowly closes.*)

THE END

Production Notes

EL CABALLITO OF SEVEN COLORS

Characters: 5 male; 4 female; 2 male or female for El Caballito.

Playing Time: 30 minutes.

Costumes: Mexican. All wear sandals. Females wear colorful skirts and peasant-style blouses, Liseta's of finer material; Liseta also wears a mantilla, a flower in her hair, dangle earrings, a Spanish shawl, and carries a fan; Madre and Servants wear white aprons. Males wear bright sashes. El Alcalde wears dark trousers, ruffled white shirt, a bolero, and a felt sombrero. Padre, Carlos, Luis, and Juan wear white trousers (pajama-like), white shirts, and serapes; Padre initially wears a straw sombrero, given later to Juan. El Caballito (2 people) has a horse head (papier-mâché with a yarn mane), a tube-like central section made of a sheet, holes left for legs, and a flowing yarn tail, the entire outfit painted with seven colors, some phosphorescent to glow in night scenes.

Properties: Guitar, five signs (as indicated in script), two eaten-clean corncobs, rope, book, flowers, snake and old-man hand puppets, rattle.

Setting: Dark backdrop curtain. Scene 1: Cardboard cutouts of ten cornstalks, chair. Scene 2: Cardboard cutout of large cactus. The balcony in Before Rise, Scenes 2 and 3, is a low, three-sectional, cardboard cutout painted to look like wrought iron.

Lighting: Blackouts at times indicated in Scene 1; for night scenes, dim lights and possibly add a blue flood, spot on area where brothers sit; regular lights for other scenes.

Sound: Rooster crowing, crickets (amplify clicker or use recording); horse eating corn (amplify crushing piece of paper); if desired, Juan may mime to recorded songs; dance music for Scene 3 (recorded).

The Ghost of El Castillo

Tales abound of ghosts who continue to haunt the world because of some wrong they did in life. What makes this tale particularly interesting is that the person who gets rid of the ghost is a tinker, whose job in life is repairing what other people break. He is not the wisest man nor the strongest, but he knows a few simple truths and applies them.

In the past, this tale was most often told in the Extremadura, a region in central Spain where the landscape is bleak and desolate with extremes of temperature, a place where often it is a struggle to stay warm in the winter and cool in the summer, where castles with thick stone walls were built on top of rocky hills, and where food was not always plentiful. From this region came many of the conquistadors, seeking adventure and a new chance in life.

In most versions of this tale, the Condesa's husband is killed and dismembered by bandits and ghostly body parts keep falling into the castle halls, frightening all except the brave tinker who manages to piece the body back together so that the ghost can tell him what is wrong. To recreate this on the stage seemed too difficult. Besides, with such murderous conditions in many areas of the world these days, who needs more flying body parts?

The Ghost of El Castillo

Characters

ESTEBAN, *a tinker*
CHILDREN, *extras*
JUANITA
LOLA
SEÑORA MORO, *an innkeeper*
THE CONDESA, *owner of the castle*
YOUNG VILLAGER
VILLAGE ELDER
THE GHOST

SCENE 1

TIME: *A morning long ago.*
SETTING: *Village square in central Spain. Backdrop (reversible, three-panel screen) painting of village with bleak hill right topped by gray castle. Cork tree cutout shades bench left.*
AT RISE: *LOLA is sweeping down left. ESTEBAN enters right, beating pan with spoon. LOLA, smiling, watches him pass.*

ESTEBAN (*Shouting*): All with broken pans come to me. I, Esteban the tinker, will mend your wares. All with broken pans, come to me. I, Esteban the tinker, (*Throws LOLA a kiss which she returns, then exits down left, voice fading out*) will mend your wares. (CHILDREN, *holding hands in chain fashion, enter right, and skip around bench, chanting.*)

CHILDREN (*In unison*):
  We have heard a restless voice
  Moan and cry, groan and sigh.
  We have seen an eerie light
  Grow and beam, glow and gleam.
  (*Drop hands and face audience*)
  If you dare
  (*Point to castle*)
  To go up there
  (*Point to audience*)
  We think you might
  (*Hit chest, bend knees*)
  Die of fright.
  (*Look mysterious*)
  For in that castle is the most
  (*Shiver as if scared*)
  Extraordinary
  (*Pause, then jump at audience and yell*)
  Ghost!
  (*Burst into laughter and exit up left, running, giggling.*
  JUANITA, *with small jar, wearily enters up right.*)
JUANITA (*Wiping sweat from face*): *Buenos días*, Lola.
LOLA: *Buenos días*, Juanita. You look hot and tired.
JUANITA: *Sí.* (*Sits on bench*) *Muy* hot and *muy* tired.
LOLA: Where have you been?
JUANITA: Gathering saffron on the hill. (*Gestures at hill*)
LOLA (*Gasps*): Did you go near *El Castillo*?
JUANITA: No. I am not foolish. I went as far as the crocus field, gathering enough saffron to flavor two months of *paellas*.
LOLA (*Sitting on bench*): I wouldn't go near *that* castle. Who knows, the ghost may be roaming the hill.
JUANITA: Not in daylight. It appears only at night.
LOLA: Maybe so, but I'm not taking any chances.

JUANITA: Nor is the Condesa. She hasn't gone near the castle since that terrifying night two weeks ago when the groaning and wailing began. The sounds were so horrifying that the servants fled, and the Condesa ran screaming from the castle.

LOLA (*Nodding knowingly*): Sí. That was the night after her husband died.

JUANITA: It is his unhappy spirit, no doubt about it.

LOLA: Now the Condesa spends her nights in a little room at our inn and her days staring at her castle. Every morning when I bring her coffee, she looks sadder than the day before.

JUANITA (*Staring at castle*): I hope the evil spirit can soon be exorcised.

LOLA: Exorcised? What does that mean?

JUANITA: Gotten rid of, banished, sent back among the dead.

LOLA (*Nodding*): Ah, (*Nods*) sí, ex-or-cised. (SEÑORA MORO, *with cane, enters down left, sees* LOLA.)

SEÑORA MORO (*Shaking cane at her*): Lola! (LOLA *jumps.* JUANITA *grimaces.*) From my balcony I saw you making eyes and throwing a kiss to Esteban the tinker.

LOLA: But, Señora Moro, I love Esteban. Some day, if we ever have enough money, we hope to be married.

MORO: A *señorita* should never throw kisses. Shame on you. And now you waste your time gossiping with Juanita.

LOLA (*Shaking head*): I wasn't gossiping. I was just resting for a very few minutes.

MORO: Ha! Well, hurry back to the inn. The patio must be swept, the Condesa has finished her coffee, and there are dishes to wash. (*Waves cane*) ¡Escurite!

LOLA (*Curtsying*): Sí, señora. (*Exits down left, running.* JUANITA *rises and warily backs away from* MORO.)

JUANITA: *Buenos días,* Señora Moro. (*Holds up jar*) I worked hard today. I rushed out at dawn to collect saffron, and now I am going to go home to, ah, (*Thinks hard*) clean the house.

MORO: *Bueno.* People who squander time are as useless as crows. (*Waves cane*) ¡*Escurite!* (JUANITA *scurries away, exiting up left.* MORO *sinks onto bench. To audience*) Since I own the largest inn in town, I have experience giving orders. (*Leans forward, smiling mischievously*) But I pick only on lazy people. (*Cackles crow-like at her cleverness.* THE CONDESA *enters sadly down left, gazes at castle and sighs.*)

CONDESA: Ah, me!

MORO: Condesa, staring at your castle won't scare the ghost away. Come sit beside me. Perhaps we can devise a plan. (CONDESA *sighs again as she sits on bench.*)

CONDESA: Oh, Señora Moro, if only I knew how to ease my husband's spirit, then I'm sure it would no longer haunt the castle.

MORO: Why is the ghost so unhappy?

CONDESA: Because when my husband was alive he was a greedy man. He forced the poor people in his district to pay heavy taxes; he gave nothing to the church; and he never helped a person in need. He always meant to change, but he never did.

MORO: No wonder his spirit is miserable.

CONDESA (*Nodding*): *Sí.* The priest has tried with no success to exorcise the ghost from the castle. I fear my husband will haunt those halls forever, and I will never be able to go back home.

MORO: Why not offer a reward? Surely someone will have a solution.

CONDESA (*Throwing up arms*): *Sí.* An excellent idea. (CHILDREN *reenter left, holding hands as before, skipping and chanting.*)

CHILDREN (*In unison*):

We have heard a restless voice
Moan and cry, groan and sigh.
We have seen an eerie light
Grow and beam, glow and gleam.

MORO (*Rising, waving cane authoritatively*): Attention, children! The Condesa wishes to make an announcement. Listen carefully, then proclaim her words to everyone in the village.

CHILDREN (*In unison, curtsying, nodding*): Sí, señora.

CONDESA (*Rising, raising arms*): To the person who banishes the ghost from *El Castillo*, I offer a reward of one thousand gold *reales*. (*Others gasp in wonder then freeze. Curtain*)

* * * * *

SCENE 2

BEFORE RISE: CHILDREN *skip across from right to left in front of curtain, chanting.*

CHILDREN (*In unison*):
Banish the ghost from *El Castillo*,
If you be so bold.
The Condesa then will pay you
A thousand *reales* of gold. (*Repeat verse, exiting left, voices fading out.* YOUNG VILLAGER, *with sword, enters right followed by* VILLAGE ELDER, *with book, hobbling.*)

YOUNG VILLAGER: A thousand gold *reales*! I could use that money to take all of my friends on a fancy holiday.

VILLAGE ELDER: I could use that money to build a bigger house and buy a dozen donkeys, one for each member of my family.

YOUNG VILLAGER: Because I am young and strong,

I should go first. With my sword (*Flashes it*) I will banish that evil spirit.

VILLAGE ELDER: You may go first. But, since I am old and wise, I have the best chance to succeed. Instructions from a book (*Holds it up*) will exorcise the ghost. (VILLAGERS *exit, ad libbing: "I am stronger than you," "I'm wiser than you," etc., fading out. ESTEBAN enters left, beating pan, crossing right.*)

ESTEBAN (*Shouting*): All with broken pans come to me. I, Esteban the tinker, will mend your wares. (*Stops and speaks to audience*) Should those two villagers (*Points left with thumb*) fail, I, Esteban the tinker, will try to rid the castle of the ghost. With a thousand gold *reales*, finally I would be rich enough to marry my sweetheart, Lola. (*Beats pan, shouts as he exits left, voice fading out*) All with broken pans come to me. (*Blackout. CHILDREN chant from off stage.*)

CHILDREN (*In unison*):
The young man came, his chest puffed out,
Full of strength and boast,
He waved his sword and shouted loud
To exorcise the ghost. (*Curtain opens.*)

* * *

TIME: *Late that night.*

SETTING: *Inside castle. Backdrop screen reversed, revealing gray stone wall. Lights dim; moonlight shines on bench area, which is moved to castle. No tree. Sound of howling wind now and then.*

AT RISE: YOUNG VILLAGER *sits on bench, shivering, sword in hand. He looks about furtively.* GHOST *is behind backdrop.*

YOUNG VILLAGER (*To audience; nervously*): The winds howl outside the castle. I am cold and hungry. For three hours I have waited and nothing ghostly has happened. However, it is almost midnight—a likely time for the spirit to appear. (*Clock bongs 12 times;* YOUNG VILLAGER *grows more fearful with each bong.*)

GHOST (*Wailing from behind backdrop*): ¡Ay-y-y-y-y!

YOUNG VILLAGER (*Leaping to feet, sword ready*): It is the ghost.

GHOST (*Wailing louder*): Woe-o-o-o!

YOUNG VILLAGER (*Looking about wildly, calls*): Where are you? (GHOST *bursts onto stage, waving arms in a mysterious way.*)

GHOST (*In spooky voice*): Here-r-r-r, there-r-r-r-r-r, everywhere-r-r-r-r-r.

YOUNG VILLAGER (*Terrified, leaping on bench, shouting*): ¡Ay caramba! (GHOST *slowly approaches* YOUNG VILLAGER, *moaning and swaying.*)

GHOST (*Howling*): Oh-h, misery! Oh-h-h, agony! Oh-h-h, woe!

YOUNG VILLAGER (*Frantically slicing air with sword*): Ghost, I will dispatch you, eliminate you, send you back to your grave.

GHOST (*Crying maniacally*): Wa-a-a! You cannot hurt a ghost. Eee-e-e-e! (*Continues forward*)

YOUNG VILLAGER (*Frightened*): Come no closer! (*Leaps from bench, backing up right, sword raised defensively*) ¡Alto! ¡Alto! (GHOST *continues toward* VILLAGER, *who shrieks.*) No! No! (*Bolts off stage, screaming*) Help! Help! I give up! (*Blackout. After a pause* CHILDREN *chant from off stage.*)

CHILDREN (*In unison*):
The elder brought a book of knowledge,
It seemed to him quite clear
That if he followed rules of logic,
The ghost would disappear. (*Lights come back up dimly.*)

* * *

TIME: *Late the next night.*
SETTING: *Same as before.*
AT RISE: VILLAGE ELDER, *with book, sits shivering on bench.*

VILLAGE ELDER (*To audience*): I am hungry and cold. I would like nothing better than to eat a bowl of hot stew and then climb into my warm bed. Oh, well, this ordeal will soon be over. Last night the foolish young villager tried to banish the ghost by force. I knew that would not work. (*Matter-of-factly*) Tonight I will explain to the ghost why it cannot stay here. (*Clock strikes 12.* VILLAGE ELDER *looks more nervous with each bong.*)

GHOST (*Wailing*): ¡Ay-y-y-y-y!

VILLAGE ELDER (*Rising, scared*): It is the ghost.

GHOST (*Wailing louder*): Woe-o-o-o!

VILLAGE ELDER (*Looking about wildly, calls*): Where are you? (GHOST *bursts on stage, waving arms.*)

GHOST: Here-r-r-r-r, there-r-r-r-r-r, everywhere-r-r-r-r-r-r! (VILLAGE ELDER, *terrified, stands on bench.*)

VILLAGE ELDER (*Groaning and frantically flipping through his book*): You—you listen to this! (GHOST, *swaying, moaning, slowly approaches* VILLAGE ELDER, *who reads from book in loud, shaky voice.*) People who die are laid to rest in caskets. They are buried in cemeteries. Stones mark their graves. The dead have no connection to this world.

GHOST (*Howling*): Oh-h, misery! Oh-h-h, agony! Oh-h-h-h, woe!

VILLAGE ELDER (*Shouting*): Ghost, listen to knowledge and logic. You do not belong among the living.

GHOST (*Crying maniacally*): Wa-a-a! You cannot teach a ghost. Ee-e-e-e! (*Continues forward*)

VILLAGE ELDER (*Frightened*): ¡Madre Dios! Come no closer! (*Climbs down from bench, nearly falling, and backs away right, book raised defensively*) ¡Alto! ¡Alto! (GHOST continues toward VILLAGE ELDER, *who shrieks.*) No! No! (*Hobbles right as fast as he can, screaming*) Help! Help! I give up. (*Blackout.* VILLAGE ELDER *exits. After a pause* CHILDREN *chant from off stage.*)

CHILDREN (*In unison*):
The tinker cooked himself some soup.
He was not afraid.
Determination, warmth, and food—
Of such is courage made. (*Lights come up dimly.*)

* * *

TIME: *Late the next night.*
SETTING: *Same as before. Fake fire down right of bench.*
AT RISE: ESTEBAN, *with pan and spoon, sits on floor, leaning against bench; pantomimes eating from pan.*

ESTEBAN (*To audience*): The sword and the book were not successful. A sword may be necessary for defense, and a book can point the way in life, but neither can make a person brave or banish a ghost. I built a fire in the fireplace, (*Gestures*) so I am warm; I cooked garlic soup, (*Holds up pan*) so my stomach is full. It is difficult to be brave when cold and hungry. (*Rises*) What is even more important is determination. I will not be afraid. As for the ghost, if I am not frightened, I think I can find a way to make it disappear. (*Clock strikes 12 times.* ESTEBAN *eats a spoonful of soup and sits on bench.*)

GHOST (*Wailing*): ¡Ay-y-y-y-y-y!

ESTEBAN: Hm-m, that must be the ghost. (*Leaves spoon in pan, sets it on bench and listens attentively*)

GHOST: Woe-o-o-o-o-o!

ESTEBAN: What a sad sound! That ghost must be terribly unhappy. (*Calls*) Where are you? (GHOST *bursts on left, waving arms.*)

GHOST: Here-r-r-r-r-r, there-r-r-r-r-r, everywhere-r-r-r-r-r!

ESTEBAN: Indeed. Well, *buenas noches* to you. (GHOST *slowly approaches* ESTEBAN, *moaning and swaying.*)

GHOST (*Howling*): Oh-h, misery! Oh-h-h, agony! Oh-h-h-h, woe!

ESTEBAN (*Rising, inspecting ghost*): In truth, I have never heard such sorrow.

GHOST (*Crying maniacally*): Wa-a-a! Ee-e-e-e-e! (*Continues forward.* ESTEBAN *folds arms contemplatively and holds ground.*)

ESTEBAN: Are you the ghost of the Condesa's husband?

GHOST (*Wailing*): I am that woeful one. (*Bows head, swaying, groaning*) Oh-h-h, how I long to be away from here. My spirit is so-o-o-o anguished.

ESTEBAN: That's too bad. Well, I'm rather good at making things better. You see, I am a tinker. I mend what is broken, fit pieces together, take wrongs and make them right.

GHOST (*Incredulously*): Would you-o-o-o-o help a ghost? No-o-o-o-body before has been so bra-a-a-ve.

ESTEBAN (*Nodding*): I'd be happy to help you. What can I do?

GHOST (*Floating about, moaning*): Beneath a stone in the castle courtyard lies a trea-a-a-sure. (*Hands on head, swaying*)—money I sto-o-o-o-ole and hoar-r-r-r-d-ed during my li-i-i-fe.

ESTEBAN: What shall I do with your money?

GHOST (*Stopping, extending arms forward*): Gi-i-i-ve it to the church. Tell them three quarters must go to the poor. (*Clutches arms, sways*) Then-n, my tortured spirit can rest; then-n-n, I will no longer haun-au-nt *El Castillo.* Then-n-n, I can leave this world behi-i-ind. (*Whirls*) ¡Ay! ¡Ay!

ESTEBAN (*Picking up pan, spoon*): Poor ghost. Lead me

to your treasure. I will do as you say. (GHOST *exits left, moaning, arms outstretched, followed by* ESTEBAN. *Curtain*)

* * * * *

SCENE 3

SETTING: *Same as Scene 1.*
AT RISE: LOLA *and* ESTEBAN *stand center;* YOUNG VILLAGER, JUANITA, *and* VILLAGE ELDER *stand right;* SEÑORA MORO *sits on bench,* THE CONDESA *standing beside her.* CHILDREN *skip on right, chanting, holding hands as before, weaving in and out of crowd.*)

CHILDREN (*In unison*):
　Esteban helped the ghost,
　He fixed his troubled heart,
　Esteban, by being kind,
　Made the ghost depart.
ALL (*Ad libbing*): The brave tinker. Esteban is so clever! He got rid of the ghost. (*Etc.*)
MORO (*Rising, shouting with upraised arms*): Quiet, everybody! The Condesa wishes to speak. (CHILDREN *sit on ground facing* CONDESA. MORO *sits on bench. All quiet, focused on* CONDESA.)
CONDESA (*Speaking to crowd*): As we have learned, my husband's troubled spirit could not be soothed by the strength of youth, (*All nod in agreement;* YOUNG VILLAGER *shrugs.*) nor by the wisdom of old age. (*All nod;* VILLAGE ELDER *shrugs.*) Help for my husband's ghost came from the compassion and ingenuity of Esteban, the brave tinker, who found the way to heal a broken heart. For this I reward Esteban with 1,000 gold *reales* and my eternal gratitude. (*All cheer.*)
MORO (*Rising*): Esteban, you have my permission to marry Lola. And Lola, you'd better marry him quickly

before some other *señorita* catches him. (*All laugh and clap as* LOLA *curtsies to* ESTEBAN, *who takes her hand and bows to her.* CHILDREN *jump up, and come down center, joining hands, facing audience, chanting, while others freeze.*)

CHILDREN (*In unison*):
Soon Esteban and Lola
Were married, man and wife.
May *El Castillo's* ghostly tale
Help you (*Arms forward*) with your life. (*Curtsy. Then, others curtsy or bow. Curtain*)

THE END

Production Notes

THE GHOST OF EL CASTILLO

Characters: 4 male; 4 female; extras for Children.

Playing Time: 25 minutes.

Costumes: Traditional Spanish. Esteban, Young Villager, and Village Elder are dressed poorly; Lola wears an apron. Señora Moro carries a cane, and she and the Condesa wear fancy shawls and *mantillas*. Children are barefoot. Ghost appears in sheet with holes for eyes, nose, and mouth.

Properties: Broom, pan, spoon, small jar filled with imitation saffron, sword, large book, fake fire (cardboard cutout, crushed red cellophane attached to top, flashlight shining up to simulate flames).

Setting: Three-part, reversible screen hinged with fabric, each section about three feet wide and six feet high, and set up so sides angle slightly down stage. One side of screen has painting of village, bleak hill and castle above it on right; opposite side has painting of gray stone castle wall. Small bench and cardboard cutout of cork tree.

Lighting: For Scene 2, dim lights with a blue flood for added effect and a spot on bench area to simulate moonlight.

Sound: Background sound (so as not to interfere with dialogue) of howling wind, intermittent during Scene 2.

The Great Hurricane

Most cultures have tales about tricksters: usually a weak, little animal or person cleverly outwits a larger, more ferocious animal or person. Often, the same tales are told in different cultures, using different tricksters and settings, and often there are as many versions as there are storytellers.

In a number of cultures the trickster is a rabbit. Numerous tales in East Africa tell us how Hare fools Elephant, Lion, Leopard, or Crocodile. African slaves in the Americas told stories about Brer Rabbit. In Mexico, Rabbit tricks Coyote or Fox. In Puerto Rico, Rabbit outsmarts Tiger.

Tigers are not native to Puerto Rico, nor to Africa, nor to the Americas, where there are versions of the same tales. It is possible the roots come from Asia, where the tiger lives. In African stories leopards are sometimes referred to as tigers, as are the jaguars in Central and South American tales.

Environmental problems of a culture are reflected in its old tales. In the savannahs of East Africa, where having enough water is a prime concern, the setting is often at a water hole or by a river; in India, where floods and other disasters periodically wipe out crops, food is often the subject matter. Thus it is that in the Caribbean, where hurricanes occur with terrifying devastation, many folktales deal with the weather.

The Great Hurricane

Characters

LA GALLINITA, *the little hen*
EL CONEJO, *the rabbit*
EL TIGRE, *the tiger*
LA COQUI, *the small tree frog*
EL PAPAGAYO, *the parrot*

SETTING: *Backdrop shows mountains of Puerto Rico; banana and palm trees, hanging vines, and part of a sugarcane field appear to continue off right. Left center is a large tamarind tree.*

AT RISE: *Sound of bongo drums is heard from offstage as* LA GALLINITA *rushes on left, clucking and appearing frightened. Noise is heard from off left, and she flutters about, then hides behind sugarcane, up right.* EL CONEJO *enters right, carrying coiled rope, dancing to drumbeat with rabbit-like spring.* LA GALLINITA *sees him and, obviously sighing in relief, crosses to tree, left, and sinks wearily under it.* EL CONEJO *bows to her as she crosses. Drum fades out.* NOTE: *Similar drumbeats are heard throughout all entrances and exits. During dialogue,* LA GALLINITA *always clucks when speaking and* EL CONEJO *always twitches nose.*

GALLINITA: It is only you, El Conejo. I am relieved. But what is a rabbit doing with a rope?
CONEJO: I thought it might be useful sometime. I made it out of vines. (*Throws it down. At sound,* LA

33

GALLINITA *jumps and squawks.*) La Gallinita, little hen, you seem frightened of everything.

GALLINITA: *Sí, sí!* I have had a miserable morning! El Tigre, the terrible tiger, caught two of my friends, and I barely got away.

CONEJO: I know how you feel. Much of my life is spent running from El Tigre. (*Slow drumbeat begins. EL TIGRE enters unseen and pads, catlike, across stage to hide behind sugarcane. Drum ceases. EL TIGRE peers out at animals, licking lips.*)

GALLINITA: A rabbit like you (*Gesturing to him*) can hop away and hide under ground. (*Gesturing*) I have spindly legs that won't travel quickly. And I can't fit into a hole the way you can, nor hide among roots and leaves like little Tree Frog. And, although I have feathers I cannot fly like the Parrot. (*Waves wings*)

CONEJO: Then you must use your brains, Little Hen. A clever trick will often fool the mightiest of creatures.

GALLINITA: True. But I am not as clever as you. (*EL TIGRE sneaks across to tree and peeks out, flexing claws and exercising jaws.*) Wise, slippery Culebra, the snake, has often said that you are the cleverest animal in Puerto Rico. (*EL TIGRE gestures "no."*)

CONEJO (*Modestly*): I don't think that is entirely correct. I do have more sense than that silly Tiger, though! (*EL TIGRE roars in indignation. EL CONEJO and LA GALLINITA momentarily freeze in terror. Then, as they start to run in opposite directions, EL TIGRE leaps between them, grasping each with a paw on the head. They freeze again.* NOTE: *EL TIGRE always speaks with a snarling, nasty tone.*)

TIGRE: Little Rabbit, what did you say about a silly tiger?

CONEJO: Nothing, nothing. I meant to say, "Sharp Tiger," as sharp as your claws. (*EL TIGRE nods and smiles. LA COQUI hops on right, chirping happily. Sud-*

denly she sees EL TIGRE *and jumps and squeaks in fright, starting to hop off right.* EL TIGRE *snarls.*)

TIGRE: La Coqui! Stop! (LA COQUI *freezes.* NOTE: *She always speaks in a high voice.*)

COQUI (*Trembling*): El Tigre, what could you possibly want with a small tree frog like me? I wouldn't even make a proper mouthful.

TIGRE: Today I want you only as my messenger.

COQUI (*Nodding*): Sí, sí.

TIGRE: Go tell slippery Culebra, the snake, that I am having Hen and Rabbit for supper. She thinks the rabbit is the cleverest animal. Now she will change her mind! (EL CONEJO *looks about fearfully, then puts paw to brow, as if thinking.*)

COQUI (*Nodding*): Sí, sí.

TIGRE: Then hop back here and tell me what she says to that.

COQUI: Sí, sí.

TIGRE (*Roaring*): Now, *vamos!* Go before I change my mind and swallow you.

COQUI (*Hopping right*): Sí, sí, sí, sí. . . . (*Exits*)

TIGRE: And now—my supper! (*Licks lips and opens mouth*)

CONEJO: El Tigre! Wait! I am glad you are going to eat us. (EL TIGRE *sits, puzzled, letting others go.*)

GALLINITA (*Tearfully*): I'm not glad.

TIGRE (*To* EL CONEJO): Why are you glad I will eat you?

CONEJO: Because soon a horribly unpleasant, long-suffering end will come for everyone.

TIGRE: What end?

CONEJO: A great hurricane is going to strike this island at any moment.

GALLINITA (*Surprised*): ¡Caramba!

TIGRE: I have heard nothing about a hurricane.

CONEJO: Of course not. You have been too busy chasing us poor creatures to know anything.

TIGRE (*Slyly*): Who told you a great hurricane was coming?

CONEJO: El Papagayo, the parrot.

GALLINITA: He should know. That bird flies everywhere, investigating everything.

TIGRE (*Still not quite convinced*): I refuse to believe it.

CONEJO: Suit yourself. (*Dramatically*) This will be the worst storm in the history of the Caribbean Sea.

GALLINITA (*Squawking in alarm*): ¡Caramba! I'd rather be eaten.

CONEJO (*Gesturing wildly*): Palm trees will be uprooted. Banana leaves will blow away. Sugarcane will be swept flatter than a chile omelet. All the animals will be thrown into the deep, churning, crashing sea. (LA GALLINITA *bursts into frightened clucking, fluttering wings.* EL TIGRE *bites claws and looks nervously at sky.*)

TIGRE (*Waving claws*): I won't let the hurricane come here!

CONJEO (*Louder*): The only thing that will survive is this (*Pointing*) strong tamarind tree. (EL TIGRE *rushes to clutch tree.*)

TIGRE: I'll be saved. I'll be saved.

CONEJO: The wind will blast with the force of a thousand tigers. It will rip you off the tree and toss you in the air as if you were a butterfly. (*Paws to ears*) Listen. I think I hear the hurricane coming now. (LA GALLINITA *runs about squawking;* EL TIGRE *gestures frantically and looks at sky.*)

TIGRE (*Shouting*): Help, help! Save me!

CONEJO (*Loudly*): La Gallinita, don't be afraid. I will save you. (*Picks up rope*) I will tie you to the tamarind tree so you will not be blown away.

GALLINITA (*Tearfully*): Gracias, amigo, but I cannot

allow you to sacrifice yourself. (*Takes rope*) I will tie *you* to the tree.

CONEJO (*Taking rope*): No, little Hen. You have been a good friend. Let me tie *you* to the tree.

GALLINITA: No, let me. (*Takes rope*)

TIGRE (*Roaring*): No, no! *I* shall be the one tied to the tamarind tree! (*Puffing up*) El Tigre will survive the hurricane. (*To* LA GALLINITA) Tie me up.

GALLINITA: Why should I? You're no friend of mine.

TIGRE: Tie me to the tree or I'll eat you *pronto*.

GALLINITA: It's all over for me either way. I refuse. (*Drops rope and crosses "wings" with determination*)

TIGRE (*Whining*): El Conejo, *amigo*, let us be friends. Do one kind deed in your short remaining life. Please, I beg of you, tie me to the tree.

CONEJO (*Picking up rope with sigh*): All right, although why I should do you a favor is hard to understand. (*Ties* EL TIGRE *to tree*) There.

TIGRE: *Gracias, Señor. Gracias.* I shall never forget your kindness.

CONEJO (*Dramatically*): *Adíos.* (*Waves*) I shall meet my end as bravely as I can. (*Staggers off left.* LA GALLINITA *sits center, clucking nervously, wings in prayerful attitude.* EL TIGRE *stares at sky and cocks ear, trying to hear hurricane.*)

TIGRE: Strange. I cannot hear the hurricane coming. (EL PAPAGAYO *enters right, swooping as if flying, screeching in surprise as he sees* EL TIGRE *and* LA GALLINITA. NOTE: EL PAPAGAYO *always screeches between sentences.*)

PAPAGAYO: What is going on here?

GALLINITA: We are waiting for the hurricane, El Papagayo.

PAPAGAYO: What hurricane?

TIGRE: The one that will destroy everything on the island except me.

PAPAGAYO: There is no storm coming.

GALLINITA: Rabbit said you said a hurricane was coming.

PAPAGAYO: I most certainly did not say that. Why, it isn't even hurricane season.

TIGRE (*Roaring*): What? What? No hurricane? Not even hurricane season? (*Growls furiously and claws at sky*) El Conejo played a trick on me. Parrot, come here! Untie me at once! *¡Pronto! ¡Pronto!* (EL PAPAGAYO *unties him, leaving rope beside tree. Meanwhile,* LA GAL-LINITA *cackles with laughter.*)

GALLINITA: Once again clever Rabbit tricked stupid Tiger. (*Continues laughing.* EL TIGRE, *now free, brushes* EL PAPAGAYO *away.*)

TIGRE: *Vamos,* El Papagayo. Fly away before I pull out all your feathers.

PAPAGAYO (*Indignantly*): Hmpf! What an ungrateful creature! Next time I won't lift a wing to help you. (*Exits right, swooping.* EL TIGRE *sneaks up on the still laughing* LA GALLINITA *and, as before, grasps her on head.*)

GALLINITA (*Freezing*): *¡Caramba!*

TIGRE: Now for my supper! (LA COQUI *enters right, hopping.*)

COQUI: El Tigre! (*He growls angrily.*) I told wise, slip-pery Snake that you were having Hen and Rabbit for supper.

TIGRE: And what did she say?

COQUI: She said, "Hen maybe, but Rabbit no." She doubted if you could catch El Conejo. By the way, where is Rabbit? (EL TIGRE *growls angrily and* LA COQUI *and* LA GALLINITA *tremble with fear.* EL CONEJO *peeks around edge of curtain, then springs onto stage, unseen by others, and hides behind tree. He peers out and listens.*)

TIGRE: Go tell La Culebra that I am eating Hen today and Rabbit tomorrow.

COQUI (*Nodding*): *Sí, sí.*

TIGRE: Then hop back here and tell me what she says to that. *Vamos, pronto!* (LA COQUI *hops right.*)

COQUI: *Sí, sí, sí, sí . . .* (*Exits*)

TIGRE: And now—(*Licks lips and opens mouth.* EL CONEJO *leaps forward.*)

CONEJO (*Shouting*): El Tigre! Wait!

TIGRE: El Conejo! How dare you return! You will never get a chance to trick *me* again.

CONEJO: I bring a message from wise, slippery Snake.

TIGRE: Come close and tell me.

CONEJO: I prefer to tell you from over here. The message is this: Snake claims she is far more powerful than you because she is much longer.

TIGRE (*Angrily*): What? She is not more powerful, and she is not longer.

CONEJO: That's exactly what I told her, but she won't believe me. She said, "Bring back proof that El Tigre is longer and only then will I believe he is more powerful."

TIGRE: An insult! Measure my length at once.

CONEJO: How? (*Looking about*) I could use a sugarcane as a measuring stick, but I have no knife. El Tigre, use your claws to slash off a cane.

TIGRE: All right. (*Starts to cross to cane;* LA GALLINITA *tries to sneak away.*) Little Hen! (*She freezes.*) Come with me. (*Puts paw on her head*)

GALLINITA: ¡Caramba! (*They cross to cane, right.* EL TIGRE *pantomimes slashing off piece of cane, then returns center with it, still holding on to* LA GALLINITA.)

TIGRE (*Handing sugarcane to* EL CONEJO): Here, El Conejo. Now measure me.

CONEJO: It would be easier if you would lie down. Besides, only then can you stretch out your tail to add to your length.

TIGRE: Good idea, but Little Hen must stay beside me.

CONEJO: Of course. (EL TIGRE *lies down.* EL CON-EJO *places cane on ground along* EL TIGRE's *paws, careful not to risk capture.*) Are you as long as you can possibly be, El Tigre?

TIGRE (*Stretching and grunting*): I think so.

CONEJO: It is difficult for me to measure. Keep your tail still.

TIGRE: I can't. It always flips about.

CONEJO: Then I'll use some vine rope to tie your tail to the tamarind tree so it won't get in the way. (EL TIGRE *nods.* EL CONEJO *ties one end of rope to tree, then ties loop around* EL TIGRE's *tail.*) Now stretch your front paws out this way. (*Indicates that* EL TIGRE *should stretch paws out in front of head.* EL TIGRE *does so.*) Can't you stretch any farther?

TIGRE (*Stretching and grunting*): This is as far as my paws will go.

CONEJO: But they keep sliding backward.

TIGRE: I can't help that.

CONEJO: I'll just slip this vine around under your stomach here and over your back and up here and tie your paws to the sugarcane so I can get a correct measurement. (*Picking up loose end of rope at tail, he loops it under and around* EL TIGRE's *waist, then stretches it along* EL TIGRE's *back and arms up to outstretched front paws. He secures rope to sugarcane.*) Excellent. (*Stands back*) Why, El Tigre, you truly are longer than wise, slippery Snake!

TIGRE: I told you so.

CONEJO: I shall immediately give my report to Snake.

TIGRE: *Bueno.* Good.

CONEJO: Come along, La Gallinita, help spread the

news to everyone about how powerful and clever El Tigre is. (*They exit left, hurriedly.*)

TIGRE (*Shouting*): Wait a minute! La Gallinita, come back! (*He struggles, snarling, but can't move.* EL PAPAGAYO *enters and screeches in surprise as he sees* EL TIGRE.)

PAPAGAYO: What is going on here?

TIGRE: Rabbit was measuring me, and the rope seems to have gotten tangled or something or other. Hurry up. Untie me, *pronto!*

PAPAGAYO: The last time I helped you, you weren't one bit grateful.

TIGRE: This time I will be most grateful.

PAPAGAYO: Hmpf! (LA COQUI *enters, hopping.*)

COQUI: El Tigre, I told wise, slippery Snake that you were eating Hen today and Rabbit tomorrow.

TIGRE: And what did she say?

COQUI: She didn't believe me. She said you would end up with nothing to eat. By the way, where is La Gallinita?

TIGRE (*Roaring*): Go tell wise, slippery Snake I don't like her attitude.

COQUI: *Sí.* (*Starts to exit left*)

PAPAGAYO: La Coqui, why do you keep carrying messages from Tiger to Snake and Snake to Tiger?

COQUI: So I won't get eaten.

PAPAGAYO: Look at Tiger. He is all tied up and can do no harm to you. I should think a small tree frog would be more afraid of being eaten by La Culebra, the snake. You are more her size.

COQUI: *Sí!* So I am. That's why I never go near her.

PAPAGAYO: But you keep bringing back messages from Snake.

COQUI: No, I don't. I just make them all up for fun.

TIGRE (*Angrily*): What? You mean, Snake never said those awful things about me?

COQUI: No. Snake has left the island. She's been gone for a week.

TIGRE: That cannot be. El Conejo said that she said— and you said that she said—(*Roars furiously*) I have been tricked by a rabbit and a tree frog! (LA COQUI *hops away.*)

COQUI: *Sí, sí, sí, sí . . .* (*Exits.* EL TIGRE *roars.*)

PAPAGAYO: Be still, El Tigre. You're making as much noise as the wind of a hurricane.

TIGRE: I am the most misunderstood creature in the forest. (*Whimpering*) Please, Parrot, untie me, and I will go away without bothering anyone again. Please, *amigo.*

PAPAGAYO: Oh, all right. After all, everyone should be free. (*Unties* EL TIGRE, *who leaps up and chases* EL PAPAGAYO *around tree, swinging rope as if to lasso him. Drum plays.*)

TIGRE (*Shouting*): Ho, ho, El Papagayo! I *am* the great hurricane, and I will blow off your feathers and eat you for supper!

PAPAGAYO (*Shrieking*): You ungrateful beast. I'll never believe you again. (*Exits noisily, pursued by* EL TIGRE. *Drums fade out and curtain closes.*)

THE END

Production Notes

THE GREAT HURRICANE

Characters: 5 male or female.

Playing Time: 20 minutes.

Costumes: Actors have faces painted to look like animals. Frog has bulges attached over eyes, Parrot and Hen have beaks, Rabbit and Tiger have whiskers. Hen has red comb attached to head. Tiger has long tail, which, if desired, can be stiffened with wire (straightened coat hanger) and attached under costume to one paw so tail may be flipped about. Rabbit and Tiger have ears stiffened with wire or cardboard. Play may be done with full, hooded costumes or with decorated faces, heads and tiger's tail only. Parrot and Hen may have feathers (made of crepe paper) attached to arms of costumes.

Properties: Rope.

Setting: Painting of Puerto Rico on backdrop, as indicated in text. Field of sugarcane, up right (sticks painted to look like sugarcane), in pots. Camouflage pots by covering area with brown wrapping paper or burlap and making holes in it through which canes protrude. Tamarind tree, left center, made of wire mesh and papier-mâché, has large trunk and appears to extend above stage with only a few branches in view of audience.

Lighting: No special effects.

Sound: Bongo drums, as indicated in text.

Brother Rabbit Sells Corn

During the 300 years of slave trade, the largest African slave population in Latin America was in Brazil, where there were 3½ million slaves or approximately 38% of the total trade shipped to the Americas. In the United States the slaves worked cotton fields; in the Caribbean and the eastern parts of South and Central America, they worked coffee and sugar plantations. A slave's life was arduous with no expectation of improvement. In spite of all the hardships, the folktales slaves brought from Africa and continued to tell had a deep current of humor and optimism.

Especially witty are the tales about small, weak, but clever Brer Rabbit who always manages to survive. Often, however, he is caught in lies and suffers when his trickery goes too far.

Brer—or Br'er—Rabbit is a short form of Brother Rabbit, and sometimes his full name is used in telling the tale. Stories about the little rabbit's exploits are found in the Southern United States, Brazil, Puerto Rico, Panama, Costa Rica, Columbia, Venezuela—wherever there were African slaves. Adaptations to the tales rose from the different environments in which the slaves were forced to live.

In Latin America, Brother Rabbit absorbed the Hispanic culture as did the black people themselves. Tales about Brother Rabbit occur in such places as corn fields, and Sister Cockroach and Señor Coyote are involved— a long way from a water hole on the African savannah where Hare met Elephant for a tug of war.

44

Brother Rabbit
Sells Corn

Characters

BROTHER RABBIT
SISTER COCKROACH
SISTER HEN
BROTHER COYOTE
HUNTER MAN

SETTING: *Countryside of Costa Rica. Down right, large rock; up right center, tree; down left, bush; up left center, hut; center, cart of corn in husks.*

AT RISE: SISTER COCKROACH *crouches behind rock;* SISTER HEN *crouches behind bush;* BROTHER COYOTE *stands behind tree;* HUNTER MAN *stands behind hut;* BROTHER RABBIT *stands beside cart.*

BROTHER RABBIT (*To audience*): This year I raised a bushel of corn in my field. It is loaded up here in my cart. (*Points to cart*) I would like to make a pile of money on this corn, and I have a plan for how best to sell it. First I will hop over and knock on Sister Cockroach's door. (*Crosses to rock and pantomimes knocking three times, accompanied by loud, offstage knocks*)
SISTER COCKROACH (*Shouting*): Who is it?
BROTHER RABBIT: Brother Rabbit.
COCKROACH: What do you want?
RABBIT: To sell you a bushel of fresh, sweet corn.

45

COCKROACH (*Peering over rock*): M-m-m-m, that sounds good.

RABBIT: It is better than good.

COCKROACH (*Looking around*): Where is this corn of yours?

RABBIT: In the middle of my field, all loaded up in my cart and waiting for you to come over and pull it away.

COCKROACH: How much are you asking for that bushel of corn?

RABBIT: Only five *colones*.

COCKROACH (*Crawling out from behind rock*): Only five *colones*?

RABBIT (*Nodding*): *Sí*. A bargain, Sister Cockroach, because you are my friend. (*Slyly*) Besides, you make good *tamales*, and I thought you might let me have a few.

COCKROACH: Sorry, Brother Rabbit. I didn't make any *tamales* today. But after I buy your corn and grind it up, I promise to make a big batch of *tamales*, and you can have a plate full.

RABBIT (*Frowning*): Don't you even have one *tamale* left now?

COCKROACH: Not a single one.

RABBIT (*Sighing*): Oh, well. (*Shrugs*) Such is the luck of a poor rabbit.

COCKROACH: But I'll come over right now and buy your corn.

RABBIT (*Quickly*): No, not now. Come to my field in (*Looks at his watch*) exactly one hour. No sooner, no later.

COCKROACH (*Nodding*): *Sí*. In one hour I'll be there. *Muchas gracias.*

RABBIT: *De nada.* (*Waves goodbye*) *Adiós*, Brother Rabbit. (*Exits, crawling back behind rock and crouching; to audience, chuckling*) That was easy. Now I will hop on over to Sister Hen's place and see what I can do there. (*Crosses to bush and pantomimes knocking three times, as loud knocks are heard from offstage.*)

SISTER HEN (*Shouting*): Who is it?

RABBIT: Brother Rabbit.

HEN: What do you want?

RABBIT: To sell you a bushel of fresh, sweet corn.

HEN (*Peering out*): M-m-m-m, that sounds good.

RABBIT: It is better than good.

HEN (*Looking around*): Where is this corn of yours?

RABBIT: In the middle of my field, all loaded up on a cart and waiting for you to come over and pull it away.

HEN: How much are you asking for that bushel of corn?

RABBIT: Only five *colones.*

HEN (*Coming from behind bush, strutting*): Only five *colones?*

RABBIT (*Nodding*): *Sí.* A bargain, Sister Hen, because you are my friend. Besides, you always cook such delicious beans, and I thought you might give me a bowl full.

HEN: Sorry, Brother Rabbit. My family finished the beans last night. Next time I cook up another pot, though, I'll invite you over.

RABBIT (*Frowning*): Don't you even have a few beans left?

HEN: Not a single one.

RABBIT (*Sighing*): Oh, well, (*Shrugs*) such is the luck of a poor rabbit.

HEN: But, I'll come over right now and buy your corn.

RABBIT (*Quickly*): No, not now. Come to my field in (*Looks at his watch*) exactly one hour and three minutes. No sooner, no later.

HEN (*Nodding*): *Sí.* In one hour and three minutes I'll be there. *Muchas gracias.*

RABBIT: *De nada.* (*Waves goodbye*) *Adiós,* Sister Hen.

(HEN *exits, strutting back behind bush and crouching.* RABBIT *scratches ear and chuckles; to audience*) I have two buyers for the same bushel of corn. I will hop on over to Brother Coyote's place and promise to sell him the corn, too. (*Crosses to tree and pantomimes knocking three times, accompanied by loud, offstage knocks*)

BROTHER COYOTE (*Shouting from behind tree*): Who is it?

RABBIT: Brother Rabbit.

COYOTE: What do you want?

RABBIT: To sell you a bushel of fresh, sweet corn.

COYOTE (*Peering around tree*): M-m-m-m, that sounds good.

RABBIT: It is better than good.

COYOTE (*Looking around*): Where is this corn of yours?

RABBIT: In the middle of my field, all loaded up on a cart and waiting for you to come over and pull it away.

COYOTE: How much are you asking for that bushel of corn?

RABBIT: Only five *colones.*

COYOTE (*Entering, slinking*): Only five *colones?*

RABBIT (*Nodding*): Sí. A bargain, Brother Coyote, because you are my friend. Besides, you make the best coffee in Costa Rica, and I thought you might give me a big cup full.

COYOTE: Sorry, Brother Rabbit. I just finished the pot of coffee, and I don't plan to make another pot until morning.

RABBIT: You don't even have half a cup sitting around some place?

COYOTE: Not a drop left.

RABBIT (*Sighing*): Oh, well. (*Shrugs*) Such is the luck of a poor rabbit.

COYOTE: But I'll come over now and buy your corn.

RABBIT (*Quickly*): No, not now. Come to my field in

(*Looks at watch*) exactly one hour and six minutes. No sooner, no later.

COYOTE (*Nodding*): *Sí.* In one hour and six minutes I'll be there. *Muchas gracias.*

RABBIT: *De nada.* (*Waves goodbye*) *Adiós,* Brother Coyote.

COYOTE (*Waving goodbye*): *Adiós,* Brother Rabbit. (*Exits, slinking back behind tree.* RABBIT *scratches ear and chuckles.*)

RABBIT: Three times I have promised to sell the same bushel of corn. Now I will hop over to the hut where Hunter Man lives and sell him the corn, too. (*Crosses to hut and pantomimes knocking three times, as knocks are heard off.*)

HUNTER MAN (*Shouting from behind hut*): Who is it?

RABBIT: Brother Rabbit.

MAN: What do you want?

RABBIT: To sell you a bushel of fresh, sweet corn.

MAN (*Peering around hut*): Where is this corn of yours?

RABBIT: In the middle of my field, all loaded up on a cart and waiting for you to come over and pull it away.

MAN (*Coming from behind hut; suspiciously*): Hm-m-m. Mighty strange you didn't bring your corn with you.

RABBIT (*Sputtering*): I—ah— wanted to make sure you'd buy it first. And I—ah— thought you would like a good morning walk.

MAN: How much are you asking for that bushel of corn?

RABBIT: Only five *colones.*

MAN: Hm-m-m. Only five *colones.* Knowing you, that price is awfully low. How come you want to sell your corn for only five *colones?*

RABBIT: Because you are my friend, Hunter Man. Besides, I thought you might give me something to eat or drink.

MAN (*Thoughtfully*): I don't mind feeding you. Sit down here, and I'll bring you a *tamale,* some beans, and a cup of coffee. (*Exits behind hut*)

RABBIT (*Sitting*): What good luck! Not only am I going to sell my bushel of corn four times, I am getting a free meal.

MAN (*Reentering with plate and cup*): Enjoy your meal. (*Hands plate and cup to RABBIT*) And while you're enjoying it, tell me what you've been doing this morning.

RABBIT (*Pantomiming gobbling food*): Well, first off I went to visit Sister Cockroach, but she didn't have any *tamales.* Then I visited Sister Hen, but she was all out of beans. (*Pantomimes slurping drink*) After that I went to see Brother Coyote, but he didn't have a drop of coffee left. So, I came over to your place, and I've had a delicious meal and a fine cup of coffee.

MAN (*Rubbing chin thoughtfully*): Hm-m-m, this morning you visited Sister Cockroach, Sister Hen, and Brother Coyote before visiting me?

RABBIT: That's right. (*Hands plate and cup back to MAN and wipes mouth with paws*)

MAN (*Nodding*): I think I understand. All right, I'll buy your bushel of corn. I'll go with you now to get it.

RABBIT (*Jumping up*): No, not now. Come to my field in (*Looks at watch*) exactly one hour and ten minutes. No sooner, no later.

MAN: One hour and ten minutes, you say?

RABBIT : *Sí, sí, Señor.* (*Waves goodbye*) *Adiós.*

MAN: *Adiós,* Brother Rabbit. (*As RABBIT crosses to stand beside cart,* MAN *walks downstage and whispers to audience.*) I know that scallywag is up to something, so I aim to show up early in his field. I'll hide behind his cart, and find out what kind of game Brother Rabbit is playing. (*Curtain*)

* * * * *

SCENE 2

TIME: *An hour later.*

SETTING: *Same as before.*

AT RISE: RABBIT, COCKROACH, HEN, *and* COY-OTE *are in same places as at start of Scene 1;* MAN *hides behind cart.* COCKROACH, *with money, enters and crawls toward cart.*

COCKROACH: *Buenos días,* Brother Rabbit.

RABBIT: *Buenos días,* Sister Cockroach. Did you bring your money?

COCKROACH (*Nodding*): *Sí.* Here. (*Hands money to* RABBIT) Now I'll pull your cart to my place, unload my corn and bring your cart right back. (*Starts to pull handle*)

RABBIT (*Peering at bush, shouts*): Wait!

COCKROACH (*Freezing*): What's the matter?

RABBIT: Here comes Sister Hen. You know how she likes to eat cockroaches. I bet she's coming here to eat you.

COCKROACH (*Shrieking*): Help! What shall I do?

RABBIT: You'd better run home and hide. I'll let you know when it's safe to come back. (COCKROACH *squeals and crawls quickly away, exits behind rock and crouches.* RABBIT *quickly pockets money.* HEN, *with money, enters and struts toward cart.*)

HEN: *Buenos días,* Brother Rabbit.

RABBIT: *Buenos días,* Sister Hen. Did you bring your money?

HEN (*Nodding*): *Sí.* Here. (*Hands money to* RABBIT) Now I'll pull your cart to my place, unload my corn and bring your cart right back. (*Starts to pull handle*)

RABBIT (*Peering at tree, shouting*): Wait!

HEN (*Freezing*): What's the matter?

RABBIT: Here comes Brother Coyote. You know how he likes to eat hens. I bet he's coming here to eat you.

HEN (*Squawking*): Help! What shall I do?

RABBIT: You'd better run home and hide. I'll let you know when it's safe to come back. (HEN, *clucking wildly, scampers away, exits behind bush and crouches. RABBIT quickly pockets money. COYOTE enters and slinks toward cart.*)

COYOTE: *Buenos días,* Brother Rabbit.

RABBIT: *Buenos días,* Brother Coyote. Did you bring your money?

COYOTE (*Nodding*): *Sí.* Here. (*Hands money to RABBIT*) Now, I'll pull your cart to my place, unload my corn and bring your cart right back. (*Starts to pull cart handle*)

RABBIT (*Peering at hut, shouting*): Wait!

COYOTE (*Freezing*): What's the matter?

RABBIT: Here comes Hunter Man. You know how he likes to shoot coyotes. I bet he's coming here to shoot you.

COYOTE (*Yelping*): Help! What shall I do?

RABBIT: You'd better run home and hide. I'll let you know when it's safe to come back. (COYOTE, *howling, dashes away and exits behind tree. RABBIT quickly pockets money, then peers again at hut, looks at his watch. Frowns*) Hunter Man is late. I wonder where he is?

MAN (*Leaping from behind cart*): Here I am!

RABBIT (*Surprised*): What are you doing here?

MAN: Listening to you sell the same bushel of corn three times and give nothing in return.

RABBIT (*Backing away, sputtering*): I—ah—I can explain everything.

MAN: Go ahead. Explain.

RABBIT: Well, my plan is to sell the corn just to you.

MAN: In that case, give me those 15 *colones* in your pocket.

RABBIT: Why?

MAN: Well, my plan is to give the money back to the creatures you cheated. Hand it over, or I'll tell on you.

RABBIT: If you tell on me, nobody will trust me again.

MAN: Why should they? You're a greedy scallywag. (*Extends hand, palm up*) The money, please.

RABBIT (*Angrily handing him the money*): Now *you* pay me five *colones* for this bushel of corn.

MAN: I already gave you the money.

RABBIT: No, you didn't.

MAN: Indeed I did.

RABBIT (*Turning pockets inside out*): Then, where is it? I don't have it.

MAN (*Laughing*): It's in your stomach.

RABBIT: In my stomach?

MAN: *Sí.* Wrapped around that *tamale* you gobbled down at my house. What a shame you didn't see the money.

RABBIT (*Clutching stomach in horror*): Oh, no, I ate my profit! (*Slaps cheeks in dismay.* MAN, *laughing, picks up handle and pulls cart off, exiting behind his hut.*) Such is the luck of a poor rabbit. (*Shrugs, to audience*) Never mind, tomorrow I will figure out another trick. (*Freezes. Curtain*)

THE END

Production Notes

BROTHER RABBIT SELLS CORN

Characters: 3 male; 2 female.

Playing Time: 20 minutes.

Costumes: Costa Rican, including shawls on females and straw hats on males, all barefoot or with sandals. Brother Rabbit has long ears (paper-covered wire) poking up through hat, tail (large powder puff), and whiskers (painted on); he wears a wrist watch. Sister Cockroach has two antennae attached to head; Sister Hen has red comb (cardboard) down the center of head, red wattle (cloth, hanging down under chin), beak (cardboard on nose attached to rubber bands hooked over ears), and tail (feather duster or curled strips of crepe paper); Brother Coyote has small, pointed ears (cardboard) sticking up through hat, long tail (rope), and whiskers (painted on).

Properties: Fake Costa Rican money (*colones*); plate and mug.

Setting: Painted backdrop of Costa Rican countryside with volcano and lush forest. Rock (brown paper over small table); bush, hut, and tree (cardboard cutouts); small stool; cart of corn (wheelbarrow or wagon covered with large wooden wheels; interior filled mostly with crumpled newspaper topped with corn in husks).

Sound: Amplified knocks as indicated in script. Costa Rican music may be used to open and close play.

Pedro De Urdemalas

One of the best-loved tricksters in Hispanic cultures is Pedro de Urdemalas (mischiefmaker), sometimes called Pedro de el Malas. He is Pedro Urdimalis in Bolivia, Pedro Tecomate in Guatemala, and El Bizarrón in Cuba. Similar tales are told in Puerto Rico, where the name Juan Bobo (fool) is used and his actions are more simple-minded. Stories about this trickster go far back in time and are thought to be Spanish in origin, although similar tales are found in other parts of Europe. By the 16th century he becomes the prototype of the *pícaro* that appears in the writings of Cervantes and other Spanish authors. Stories about Pedro the trickster were brought to the Americas and to wherever else the Spanish colonized, even to as far as the Philippines.

Many of the stories relate how Pedro outwits an oppressor—often a rich landowner or an arrogant foreigner. Scholar Aurelio Espinosa considers these tales a form of social protest. Pedro is not always honest in his trickery, and sometimes he ends up in hot water, but always he plays the role of the little man who finds a way to succeed against overwhelming odds.

Pedro de Urdemalas

Characters

JOSÉ, *a poor farmer*
MARIA, *his wife*
PEDRO DE URDEMALAS
SEÑOR MANUEL DE LOS CERDOS, *a rich pig
farmer*
SEÑORA ISABELLA, *his wife*
SEÑORITA DOLORES, *his daughter*
TWO GUESTS

SCENE 1

TIME: *Present day.*
SETTING: *Mexico, near pig ranch of Señor Manuel de Los
Cerdos. Backdrop depicts arid mountains with cactus and
mesquite trees. River is assumed below stage; swamp down
left. Cardboard cutouts of row of spindly corn stalks up left;
mesquite tree right.*
AT RISE: JOSÉ *and* MARIA, *both barefoot, hoe weeds
around corn.* PEDRO DE URDEMALAS, *weary and hot,
also barefoot, enters right, not seeing* JOSÉ *or* MARIA.
He falls to knees at river. JOSÉ *and* MARIA *lean on hoes
to watch.*

PEDRO: At last—a river. Finally I will have a drink of
water. (*Cups hands and pantomimes drinking, then rises
and sinks down under tree, removes hat and wipes sweat
from face*) I am so hot and tired. I have walked ten
miles today.

JOSÉ (*Calling*): *Buenas tardes, señor.* Who are you, and where are you from?

PEDRO (*Noticing him*): I am Pedro de Urdemalas, and I come from everywhere.

JOSÉ (*Puzzled*): From everywhere?

PEDRO (*Rising wearily*): So it seems. I wander around Mexico, working here and there. And what is your name, *señor*?

JOSÉ: José. I am a poor farmer with only a small patch of corn to keep my family alive. This is my good wife, Maria.

PEDRO (*Removing hat and bowing*): *Buenas tardes* to you both.

JOSÉ: Have you come to our valley to find work?

PEDRO (*Nodding*): *Sí.* Right now I have no money. (*Turns pockets inside out*) See how it is? (*Sighs*) This is a big problem, as, unfortunately, a person must eat to stay alive. Furthermore, my feet are sore. (*Indicates feet*) It would be good to have enough money to buy a pair of sandals.

MARIA: You might find a job at the *hacienda* over there. (*Points off left*)

PEDRO: A good suggestion. (*Starts to cross left*)

JOSÉ (*Quickly crossing to* PEDRO): Careful, *señor.* (*Points to swamp*) Don't walk into that deep, smelly swamp by the river. Nobody would hire you then.

PEDRO (*Examining swamp, sniffing*): *Sí.* The mud here is indeed deep and smelly. *Gracias* for the warning. Now, tell me about the owner of the *hacienda.* What is his name?

JOSÉ: Señor Manuel de los Cerdos.

MARIA (*Crossing to* PEDRO): He is a rich, greedy man. He won't pay you much.

PEDRO: You know this for a fact?

MARIA (*As if afraid to be overheard*): *Sí.* We have watched him get wealthier and wealthier, yet he helps nobody outside his family. His wife and daughter are the same way.

PEDRO: How did this *señor* get so rich?

JOSÉ: He started out with 50 pigs, had 25 butchered and sold the pork. Meanwhile, the 25 pigs left had many babies. Soon he owned 100 pigs. He had 50 of those butchered and sold the pork for a higher price; the remaining pigs had babies and soon he owned 200 pigs. The pigs kept on multiplying, and he kept on selling pork, each time charging more for the meat.

MARIA: Wherever Señor de los Cerdos went, he bought pigs.

JOSÉ: He could not stand for anyone else to own pigs or to sell pork. Now he is the pig king of this valley.

MARIA (*Secretively*): His wife, Señora Isabella, and their daughter, Señorita Dolores, are just as greedy. Snooty, too.

JOSÉ (*Nodding*): Sí. The wife keeps ordering fancy necklaces for the daughter. They think they are better than anybody in this valley.

MARIA: But they are stupid ladies. Why, they don't even know how to make a *tortilla* or a *tamale*.

JOSÉ (*Shushing her*): Quiet, Maria. Here they come. (JOSÉ *and* MARIA *hurry back to hoe corn.*)

PEDRO: I shall sit under this tree and listen to these foolish women. (*Sits under tree, with hat over face, pretending to be asleep.* SEÑORA ISABELLA *and* SEÑORITA DOLORES *enter left, see* JOSÉ *and* MARIA *and turn away from them in disdain.*)

SEÑORA ISABELLA (*Gesturing*): This river is far enough for an afternoon stroll, Dolores. (*Sighs*) I do not understand why you like to take these tiresome walks.

SEÑORITA DOLORES (*In pouting childish manner*): Because, Mother dear, if I do not exercise, I might end up fat and lazy. Then no one will marry me.

ISABELLA: Ridiculous! Tomorrow important political guests from Mexico City will visit us.

DOLORES: What does that have to do with my getting married?

ISABELLA: They are considering your father for a high government position. You can be assured that if he secures that position, then you, with your beautiful necklaces and our wealth, will attract numerous bachelors.

DOLORES (*Giggling*): How exciting!

ISABELLA: We must make a good impression on these visitors. I will go to the city this afternoon and buy you a new ruby necklace.

DOLORES (*Wrinkling her nose*): But Mother, I already have a ruby necklace. And I have necklaces of gold and silver and necklaces of emeralds, diamonds, and pearls. Is there no other kind of necklace more precious than these? (PEDRO *jerks hat from face and sits up, smiling knowingly.*)

PEDRO (*In stage whisper to audience*): Ah-h-h!

ISABELLA: My dear daughter, if I could find such a necklace, I most certainly would buy it for you.

PEDRO (*Rising quickly and bowing to ladies*): Excuse me, lovely ladies. (ISABELLA *and* DOLORES *gasp and step back.*) Sorry to frighten you, but my name is Pedro de Urdemalas, and I could not help overhearing what you said. I know of a necklace more precious than anything in his world.

ISABELLA (*Haughtily*): You? How could a poor peasant like you know anything about necklaces?

PEDRO: I may be poor, but I have traveled far and seen more than most people ever see—even those who are rich.

DOLORES: Where is this necklace you say is so precious?

PEDRO: Not far away. If you meet me here tomorrow morning, I shall find the means to bring it to you. Of course, this necklace will cost you many *pesos.*

ISABELLA: How many?

PEDRO (*Rubbing chin thoughtfully*): Thirty thousand *pesos.*

ISABELLA: Money is no problem. We will meet you by the river at eleven in the morning. The necklace you speak of had better be here, and it had better be as precious as you say. Come along, Dolores. (ISABELLA *and* DOLORES *exit left.*)

JOSÉ (*Calling*): Pedro, do you know where to find such a necklace?

PEDRO (*Shaking head*): No, but I can make one. Not only that, but I know of a way to sell ten pigs to Señor Manuel de los Cerdos.

MARIA (*Astonished*): Really?

PEDRO (*Nodding*): Sí, really. But first I must know where the great *señor* has his pigs butchered.

JOSÉ (*Pointing off left, squinting*): In that pen to the right of the *hacienda.*

PEDRO (*Peering off left, squinting*): I see it. (*Gestures*) Come close, *mi amigos,* and I will tell you my plan. (JOSÉ *and* MARIA *hurry down and stand on either side of* PEDRO.) I shall collect the discarded backbones of a pig (*Holds up finger and thumb in a circle*) and string them into a necklace. (*Pokes index finger of other hand through circle to indicate stringing*)

JOSÉ: That is not a precious necklace.

PEDRO: Ah, but I can make them believe it is.

MARIA: I would love to see the haughty señorita wearing pig bones around her neck.

JOSÉ: And where will you get ten pigs to sell to Señor Manuel de los Cerdos?

PEDRO: I will bring back the discarded, twirly tails (*Makes twirly motion with index finger*) of ten slaughtered pigs.

JOSÉ: What will you do with them?

PEDRO: Plant them here. (*Points to swamp*)

JOSÉ (*Confused*): In the deep, smelly swamp?

PEDRO (*Nodding*): *Sí.* Ten tails (*Holds up ten fingers*) will turn into ten pigs. And a string of pig backbones (*Stretches out hands to indicate string*) will become a precious necklace. (*Indicates necklace around his neck*)

MARIA (*Astonished*): Really?

PEDRO (*Chuckling, shaking his head*): No, not really. You will see that those who insist on owning much more than anybody else must pay a price higher than money. (*Curtain*)

* * * * *

SCENE 2

TIME: *The next morning.*

SETTING: *Same as before, except ten pig tails protrude from the swamp.*

AT RISE: PEDRO, *pig bone necklace beside him,* JOSÉ, *and* MARIA *sit under tree eating tortillas.*

PEDRO: *Gracias* for sharing your food with me.

MARIA: We are happy to share what we have. It is not much, I'm afraid. (*Sadly indicates her tortilla*) The last of our beans are rolled up in the last of our *tortillas.*

JOSÉ: It is hard to live with so little.

PEDRO: I know this only too well. (*Looks off left and jumps to feet*) Here come Señora Isabella and Señorita Dolores. Hide behind the tree and watch what happens. (JOSÉ *and* MARIA *scramble up and hide behind tree.* PEDRO *picks up necklace, displays it to audience and smiles, then hides necklace behind him.* ISABELLA *and*

DOLORES *enter left and cross to* PEDRO, *who bows low to them.*)

ISABELLA (*Haughtily*): Well, where is it?

PEDRO: I have it here. But first let me tell you about this precious necklace. It consists of 15 priceless bones with ancient origins, stretching back to a species that existed before mankind.

DOLORES (*Intrigued*): You mean the bones on this necklace are ancient?

PEDRO: What I mean is this: Before today, no person, dead or alive, has ever viewed these bones. Also, I can say with authority that if the previous owner had not died, this necklace would not be for sale. (ISABELLA *and* DOLORES *gasp in wonder.*)

ISABELLA: Are there more necklaces like the one you have?

PEDRO: I doubt if there is another necklace like it in the world.

DOLORES (*Thrilled*): Let me see it.

PEDRO (*Presenting necklace dramatically*): A wondrous treasure!

ISABELLA (*Frowning*): It isn't very pretty.

DOLORES: But, Mother dear, it is unique. None of our important guests from Mexico City will have one like it.

ISABELLA: True.

PEDRO (*Nodding*): True, indeed.

DOLORES: And I think it would look interesting with my green silk gown and my embroidered Spanish shawl.

ISABELLA (*Contemplating*): Sí, it would look quite unique. (*To* PEDRO) Thirty thousand *pesos*?

PEDRO: Sí, I can go no lower.

ISABELLA (*Thinking a moment, then sighing; handing* PEDRO *money*): Here. (PEDRO, *with a bow, presents the necklace to* DOLORES.)

DOLORES (*Dancing off left*): I have the most precious necklace in the world. (ISABELLA, *with her nose in the air, follows* DOLORES *off.* PEDRO *grins and stuffs money under sash.*)

JOSÉ *and* MARIA (*Peeking out from tree, in unison*): ¡Caramba! (*They come out from hiding, laughing.*)

PEDRO (*Looking off left*): Here comes Señor Manuel de los Cerdos. Quickly, hide again. (JOSÉ *and* MARIA *rush back behind tree.* SEÑOR MANUEL DE LOS CERDOS, *with cane, enters left.*)

SEÑOR MANUEL (*Waving cane at* PEDRO; *arrogantly*): Pedro de Urdemalas, where are these pigs you say are for sale? I must buy them. Nobody in this valley can have pigs except me.

PEDRO (*Pointing to swamp*): There they are. Ten pigs. See, they are rooting around in the swamp.

MANUEL (*Peering at tails*): They certainly are rooting around. I cannot even see their heads.

PEDRO: You know how pigs love the mud. They seem to be having a great time in there.

MANUEL: *Sí.* I have never known pigs to have such a good time. They must be in excellent shape. How much are you asking for them?

PEDRO (*Slyly*): Thirty-five thousand *pesos.*

MANUEL (*Shaking head and waving cane*): Too much. I'll pay you no more than thirty thousand *pesos.*

PEDRO (*Considering, then throwing up arms in resignation*): Sold!

MANUEL (*Handing money to* PEDRO, *pompously*): In an hour, after I meet my influential guests from Mexico City, my workers will transport these pigs to my *hacienda.* (*Snaps fingers*) Come to think of it, I shall meet my guests here. (*Waves cane at swamp*) Then they can view the latest addition my vast herd. (*Proudly exits left.* PEDRO *grins, tucks money in sash.*)

JOSÉ *and* MARIA (*Peeking out from tree, in unison*): *¡Caramba!*

PEDRO (*Raising arms, to audience*): Now we shall hide and watch what happens to greedy, arrogant people. (*Curtain*)

* * * * *

SCENE 3

TIME: *An hour later.*

SETTING: *Same as before.*

AT RISE: *Dressed in finery,* MANUEL, *with cane,* ISA-BELLA, *and* DOLORES, *carrying pig bone necklace, enter left and cross to center.* PEDRO, JOSÉ, *and* MARIA *hide behind tree.*

MANUEL (*Squinting, peering right*): The limousine is coming.

ISABELLA (*Also squinting off right*): The driver sees us. He is stopping. (*Excitedly adjusts* DOLORES's *dress and helps her put on necklace, which* MANUEL *does not see yet.*)

MANUEL (*Waving cane and calling off right*): *Buenas tardes.* Please come here a moment. I have something interesting to show you.

DOLORES (*Giggling, calling off right*): So do I.

ISABELLA (*Remonstrating*): Dolores, calm down. You must learn to be more sophisticated.

MANUEL: They are getting out of the limousine. Here they come. (*Raises chest importantly, speaks over shoulder to* ISABELLA *and* DOLORES) I shall do the talking. You just stand there and look pretty. (TWO GUESTS *enter right.* MANUEL, ISABELLA, *and* DOLORES *bow to them.* GUESTS *bow in return.*) Welcome to my *hacienda.* Before we go to the patio for lunch, I would like to show you the latest addition to my vast herd of pigs, just to indicate how well I manage things. Why, only this morning I negotiated a clever deal, buying these (*Waves cane at swamp*) ten excellent pigs for only thirty thousand *pesos.*

1ST GUEST (*Peering*): Where are the pigs? I see only their tails.

MANUEL: The pigs are rooting around in the mud.

2ND GUEST (*Examining several tails closely*): The creatures do not appear to be moving at all.

MANUEL: They are resting a bit. Pigs needs *siestas,* too. (*Laughs artificially*) I will wake one up for you. (*Pulls a tail. To his horror, it comes out of the mud. All gasp.*) Something is wrong here. (*Angrily tosses tail aside; pulls another tail, again horrified that it comes out of the mud. All gasp again. MANUEL tosses tail aside and shouts furiously.*) Foolish pigs, you are losing your tails! Wake up, you dumb animals! Get out of that swamp. (*Rushes around and pulls out rest of tails, angrily growling and tossing tails away. All continue to gasp at each removal; GUESTS nervously back away.*)

1ST GUEST (*After last gasp*): Excuse me, Señor Manuel de los Cerdos. I do not believe there are pigs in your swamp.

MANUEL: But I paid for ten pigs. (*Angrily pokes cane here and there into swamp and shouts*) Pigs, pigs, where are you?

ISABELLA (*Shouting*): Manuel, calm down. There are no pigs in there. (*Smiles artificially to GUESTS*) My husband is playing a little joke on us.

MANUEL (*Growling*): This is no joke.

ISABELLA (*In stage whisper*): Quiet, Manuel. You are ruining our chances. (*Smiles broadly at GUESTS*) Before we go to our patio for lunch, let me show you the lovely necklace I just bought for my daughter. (*Gestures elegantly at necklace. DOLORES beams and strikes a pose.* GUESTS *warily skirt around* MANUEL *to examine necklace, then frown at each other and shrug.*)

2ND GUEST (*Clearing throat*): It is a rather strange necklace, I would say.

ISABELLA (*Proudly*): The man who sold it to me said it was made of 15 priceless bones, never before seen by anybody. There is not another necklace like it in the world.

1ST GUEST (*Nodding*): Sí. Who else would wear such a thing?

DOLORES (*Tearfully*): But don't you think it's unique?

2ND GUEST (*Nodding*): Sí, you can say that about it. (MANUEL *strides over to peer at necklace, then points at it with cane.*)

MANUEL (*Disgusted*): Those aren't precious bones. They came from the backbone of a dead pig! (*All gasp. To* ISABELLA) You fool! Who sold you this?

ISABELLA (*Alarmed*): Pedro de Urdemalas.

MANUEL: ¡Ay, caramba! (*Distraught, waves cane*) Pedro de Urdemalas! That is the same man who sold me ten pig tails. (GUESTS *furtively back away.*)

1ST GUEST (*Quietly to* 2ND GUEST): This family is *loco.*

2ND GUEST (*Quietly to* 1ST GUEST, *nodding*): Sí. A good thing we checked them out before appointing this man to the government position. Let's get out of here.

1ST GUEST (*To family*): Please excuse me. I just remembered I have an important engagement in Mexico City. I really can't stay for lunch.

2ND GUEST: Sí, sí, a big appointment. I have one, too. It was a mistake for us to come here. (GUESTS *turn and bolt off right.*)

DOLORES (*Bursting into tears*): No one will ever want to marry me. (*Throws necklace into swamp and runs off left, crying loudly*)

ISABELLA: Wait, dear daughter. Tomorrow I will buy you a huge diamond necklace. (*Runs off left*)

MANUEL (*Stamping foot and cane in disgust*): If I ever catch Pedro de Urdemalas, I will thrash him with my cane. (*To audience*) What's more, right now, I *hate* pigs. (*Exits left in a huff. PEDRO, JOSÉ, MARIA come out of hiding, laughing.*)

PEDRO: In light of what has happened, it might not be wise to ask Señor Manuel de los Cerdos for a job.

JOSÉ *and* MARIA (*Nodding, in unison*): Sí.

PEDRO (*Taking money out of sash*): Because you both helped me and shared your food, I want to split this money with you. Thirty thousand *pesos* for you (*Hands over money*), and thirty thousand *pesos* for me. (*Tucks rest of money in sash. JOSÉ and MARIA stare at money in disbelief.*)

JOSÉ (*Thrilled*): Gracias, Pedro.

MARIA (*Ecstatic*): I can't believe this good fortune. (*Runs and gives PEDRO a hug.*) Gracias, gracias.

PEDRO: You're welcome. Now I am off to see more of Mexico and to play more tricks. *Adiós, amigos.* (*Waves and exits right*)

JOSÉ *and* MARIA (*Waving, in unison*): *Adiós*, Pedro de Urdemalas. *Adiós.* (*Curtain*)

THE END

Production Notes

PEDRO DE URDEMALAS

Characters: 3 male; 3 female; 2 male or female for Guests.

Playing Time: 30 minutes.

Costumes: Mexican. Pedro and José, white shirts, pajama-type pants, sashes, sombreros, serapes; Maria, long brightly colored skirt, apron, and white peasant blouse; the three are barefoot. Isabella and Dolores, fine skirts and blouses and in Scene 3, elegant gowns (Dolores in green), fringed shawls, flowers in hair; Manuel, tight pants, frilly white shirt, bolero, and carries cane; Guests are dressed in similar fashion.

Properties: 2 hoes, tortilla (cut into 3 pieces), "pesos," "pig bone" necklace (any small, circular shape will do).

Setting: Backdrop of arid mountains with cactus and mesquite or simply a dark backdrop curtain. Cardboard cut-outs of mesquite tree and row of spindly corn stalks. For swamp, use large, flat piece of brown cardboard with 10 holes in it for pig tails (twisted wire covered with white tape).

Sound: Optional: Mexican music at start, between scenes, and at end.

Latino Trio

The first two playlets, HORMIGA'S LAWSUIT and
SEÑORITA CUCARACHA FINDS A HUSBAND are
formula tales: they follow a pattern that builds to a climax. Often in formula tales there are rhymes and
funny, repetitive sounds. These tales are popular all over
Latin America.

The story about the ant who broke her leg and
brought the lawsuit is often much longer, involving fire,
water, a cow, a knife, a blacksmith—all having a reason
why they weren't to blame for the accident. Many cultures have their own environmental variations on this
story. For example, in East Africa, storytellers tell a related version set at the water hole, using animals of
the savannah.

The little mouse who wins Miss Cockroach is often
called Peréz, and he loves onion soup. A jingle about
him falling into a pot, trying to eat the onions is chanted
by children in many Latin American countries. Sometimes Peréz marries an ant instead of a cockroach. In
Cuba, Miss Cockroach is known as Martina.

The third playlet, PEDRO'S HOLEY SOMBRERO, is
another tale about Pedro de Urdemalas, the trickster,
who, as usual, finds a way of fooling a rich man.

Latino Trio

I. HORMIGA'S LAWSUIT

Characters

JUEZ (*Judge*)
HORMIGA (*Ant*)
NIEVE (*Snow*)
SOL (*Sun*)
NUBE (*Cloud*)
VIENTO (*Wind*)
MONTAÑA (*Mountain*)
RATÓN (*Mouse*)
GATO (*Cat*)
PERRO (*Dog*)
PALO (*Small Stick*)
HOMBRE (*Man*)

SETTING: *The courtroom. Dark backdrop curtain. At center tall stool upstage of tall podium.*
AT RISE: JUEZ, *with gavel, sits on stool, studying papers.*

HORMIGA *enters left on crutches and hobbles far right, then faces* JUEZ *and bows respectfully.*
HORMIGA: Your Honor?
JUEZ (*Looking up, frowning*): What do you want?
HORMIGA: I have a lawsuit.
JUEZ (*Throwing up arms in disgust*): Even ants have lawsuits these days. (*Sighs*) State your case.
HORMIGA: I was walking along the snowy street, and

there was a place where the snow had melted. I slipped in the slush and fell, breaking two of my six legs.

JUEZ: And who do you blame for that?

HORMIGA: *La Nieve,* the snow. She should not have melted.

JUEZ (*Bellowing*): *La Nieve,* appear before the court. (NIEVE *enters left, running, stops beside* HORMIGA.)

NIEVE (*Bowing to* JUEZ): I am here, Your Honor.

JUEZ: *La Nieve,* did you melt, so that *La Hormiga* slipped and fell, breaking two of her six legs?

NIEVE: *Sí,* but it wasn't my fault. Mighty *El Sol,* the sun, shone down fiercely. I was forced to melt.

JUEZ (*Bellowing*): *El Sol,* appear before the court. (SOL *enters left, running, and stops beside* NIEVE.)

SOL (*Bowing to* JUEZ): I am here, Your Honor.

JUEZ: *El Sol,* did you shine down on *La Nieve,* so that she was forced to melt, so that *La Hormiga* slipped and fell, breaking two of her six legs?

SOL: *Sí,* but it wasn't my fault. *La Nube,* the cloud, should have passed in front of my face. Then my warmth would not have been so powerful.

JUEZ (*Bellowing*): *La Nube,* appear before the court. (NUBE *enters left, running, and stops beside* SOL.)

NUBE (*Bowing to* JUEZ): I am here, Your Honor.

JUEZ: *La Nube,* did you fail to pass in front of *El Sol,* so that *he* shone fiercely on *La Nieve,* so that *she* was forced to melt, so that *La Hormiga* slipped and fell, breaking two of her six legs?

NUBE: *Sí,* but it wasn't my fault. *El Viento,* the wind, didn't blow me in front of *El Sol.*

JUEZ (*Bellowing*): *El Viento,* appear before the court. (VIENTO *enters left, running, and stops beside* NUBE.)

VIENTO (*Bowing to* JUEZ): I am here, Your Honor.

JUEZ (*Getting exasperated*): *El Viento,* did you fail to blow *La Nube* in front of *El Sol,* so that he shone down

fiercely on *La Nieve,* so that she was forced to melt, so
that *La Hormiga* slipped and fell, breaking two of her
six legs?

VIENTO: *Sí,* but it wasn't my fault. *La Montaña,* the
mountain, stood in my way.

JUEZ (*Bellowing*): *La Montaña,* come before the court.
(MONTAÑA *enters left, running, and stops beside*
VIENTO.)

MONTAÑA (*Bowing to* JUEZ): I am here, Your Honor.

JUEZ (*More exasperated*): Did you stand in front of *El
Viento,* so he couldn't blow *La Nube* in front of *El Sol,*
so that he shone down fiercely on *La Nieve,* so that
she melted, causing *La Hormiga* to slip and fall, breaking two of her six legs? (*Blows out breath and wipes sweat
from forehead*)

MONTAÑA: *Sí,* but it wasn't my fault. If *El Ratón,* the
mouse, had nibbled the top off me, *El Viento* easily
could have blown past. (JUEZ *throws up arms in disgust.* RATÓN *enters left, running, and stops beside*
MONTAÑA.)

RATÓN (*Bowing to* JUEZ): Your Honor, I've heard the
testimony, and I object to the blame being placed on
me. I couldn't nibble off the mountain top because *El
Gato,* the cat, chased me. (GATO *enters left, running,
meowing angrily.* JUEZ *pounds gavel for silence.* RATÓN
hides behind MONTAÑA, *peering between legs.*)

GATO: Wait a minute! (*Stops behind* MONTAÑA, *speaking excitedly to* JUEZ) Your Honor, the accident wasn't
my fault. *El Perro,* the dog, chased me. (PERRO *enters,
running, barking angrily.* GATO *hisses and hides behind
stool, upsetting* JUEZ *who irately pounds gavel.* PERRO
stops in front of podium.)

PERRO (*To* JUEZ): You can't blame the accident on me.
El Palo, the stick, was after me. (PALO *enters left, glow-
ering at* PERRO, *who runs around podium.* GATO *hisses,
arching back, then rushes out.* JUEZ *again pounds gavel.*)

JUEZ (*Angrily yelling*): Silence in the courtroom!

PALO (*To* JUEZ): Your Honor, you can't blame the accident on me. *El Hombre,* the man, used me to chase (*Indicates each one*) *El Perro* who chased *El Gato,* who chased *El Ratón,* who couldn't nibble the top off *La Montaña* who stopped *El Viento* from blowing *La Nube* in front of *El Sol,* who therefore was forced to melt *La Nieve,* allowing *La Hormiga* to fall and break two of her six legs. The accident, then, is obviously the fault of *El Hombre,* the man. (*A moment of silence*)

ALL (*Bellowing*): *El Hombre!* (HOMBRE *enters left in a weary manner. He surveys group, then raises arms.*)

HOMBRE: All the problems in the world end up with me. Look, I'm sorry *La Hormiga* broke two of her six legs, and I hope she recovers soon, but I think the accident was God's fault, not mine. God made me and (*Indicates group*) the rest of you.

JUEZ: Hm-m-m, God's fault. (*Scratches chin*) Well, there is no way I can question God. (*Pounds gavel*) Case dismissed! (*Blackout. Curtain*)

II. SEÑORITA CUCARACHA FINDS A HUSBAND
(a pantomime)

Characters

NARRATOR
SEÑORITA CUCARACHA (*Miss Cockroach*)
SEÑOR GATO (*Mr. Cat*)
SEÑOR SAPO (*Mr. Toad*)
SEÑOR GALLO (*Mr. Rooster*)
SEÑOR RATÓN (*Mr. Mouse*)

TIME: *Early evening.*
SETTING: SEÑORITA CUCARACHA's *home. Center is*

balcony with archway behind, set at a slant facing left. Stage right represents inside house; stage left is outside. On small table right is fan, and presumably, items used in pantomime.
AT RISE: CUCARACHA, *inside house, pantomimes powdering nose and applying perfume behind ears, then smoothes hair, adjusts dress, examines herself in imaginary mirror, then picks up fan.* NARRATOR *enters downs right; always stands in front of curtain.*

NARRATOR: As you can see, *Señorita La Cucaracha*, the charming little cockroach, is preparing to go out onto her balcony. This is the evening she hopes to find a husband. (CUCARACHA *comes out onto balcony and peers up and down the street, taps fingers impatiently against her fan, sighs and looks sad.*) Don't be discouraged *Señorita Cucaracha*. The evening is early. (*Sees* GATO *off left.*) Ah, here comes *Señor Gato*. This cat thinks he is handsome. See how he prances? (GATO *enters left as if he is the most beautiful creature in the world.*) When *Señor Gato* sees *Señorita Cucaracha*, (GATO *freezes as he sees* CUCARACHA, *who blinks coquettishly over fan.*) he is filled with love. (GATO *grabs chest, closes eyes, groans, and reels backward.*) He cries, "Oh, beautiful *señorita*, let me marry you." (*Pantomimes*) She replies coquettishly, "Perhaps, but first I must hear you sing." (*Pantomimes*) So, *Señor Gato* takes a dramatic pose and clears his throat. (*Pantomimes*) Then, he sings as beautifully as he possibly can. (GATO, *arms outstretched, meows in loud, harsh manner.*) Oooo! *Señorita Cucaracha* cannot stand his music. (CUCARACHA *places hands over ears and squeezes up face in disgust.*) She sends him away. (CUCARACHA *disdainfully points to off right.* GATO, *paw to head in humiliation, sweeps past, exiting right.* NARRATOR *sees* GALLO *off left.*) Never mind, *Señorita Cucaracha*. Here comes *Señor Gallo*. This rooster thinks he is brave and *macho*. See how fierce he looks?

(GALLO *enters left and claws at imaginary opponents.*) When *Señor Gallo* sees *Señorita Cucaracha*, (GALLO *freezes as he sees* CUCARACHA, *who blinks as before.*) love strikes him. (GALLO *grasps his heart as if hit and collapses.*) He cries, "Oh, beautiful *señorita*, let me marry you." (*Pantomimes*) She replies coquettishly, "Perhaps, but first I must hear you sing." (*Pantomimes*) So, *Señor Gallo* flaps his wings. (*Pantomimes*) Then, he sings as beautifully as he possibly can. (GALLO, *wings outstretched, crows in loud, harsh manner.*) Oooo! *Señorita Cucaracha* cannot stand his music. (CUCARACHA *places hands over ears and squeezes up face in disgust.*) She sends him away. (CUCARACHA *disdainfully points to off right.* GALLO *struts past indignantly, exiting right.* NARRATOR *sees* SAPO *off left.*) Never mind, *Señorita Cucaracha*. Here comes *Señor Sapo*. This toad is rich. He thinks he can have anything he wants. See how he looks around for something to buy? (SAPO *enters left, peeking about in sneaky manner.*) When *Señor Sapo* sees *Señorita Cucaracha*, (SAPO *freezes as he sees* CUCARACHA, *who blinks as before.*) love creeps into his cold blood. (SAPO *shivers and collapses.*) He cries, "Oh, beautiful *señorita*, let me marry you." (*Pantomimes*) She replies coquettishly, "Perhaps, but first I must hear you sing." (*Pantomimes*) So, *Señor Sapo* squats down. (*Pantomimes*) Then, he sings as beautifully as he possibly can. (SAPO, *arms outstretched, croaks in loud, harsh manner.*) Oooo! *Señorita Cucaracha* cannot stand his music. (CUCARACHA *places hands over ears and squeezes up face in disgust.*) She sends him away. (CUCARACHA *disdainfully points to off right.* SAPO *indignantly hops past, exiting right.* NARRATOR *sees* RATÓN *off left.*) Never mind, *Señorita Cucaracha*, here comes *Señor Ratón*. This little mouse is kind and polite. He listens carefully to what everybody says. (RATÓN *enters left, scurrying, then stopping to listen.*) When *Señor*

Ratón sees *Señorita Cucaracha,* (RATÓN *freezes and studies* CUCARACHA, *who blinks as before.*) he says softly, "Oh, beautiful *señorita,* you look lonely." (*Pantomimes*) She replies, "I am." (*Pantomimes*) So, *Señor Ratón* kneels (*Pantomimes*) and serenades her. (RATÓN *squeaks out a melodic tune.*) *Señorita Cucaracha* thinks it is the loveliest music she has ever heard. (CUCARACHA *clutches chest and sighs in admiration.*) And when *Señor Ratón* kisses *Señorita Cucaracha's* hand and asks her to marry him, (*Pantomimes*) she rolls her eyes (*Pantomimes*) and says,

CUCARACHA (*Happy, loud, fan aside*): Sí. (*Blackout. Curtain*)

III. PEDRO'S HOLEY SOMBRERO

Characters

STOREKEEPER
WATCHMAKER
RICH MAN
PEDRO

TIME: *Morning.*

SETTING: *City street in Latin America. Left center, angled, is small table, two similar jackets spread out on it; right center, angled opposite way, is small table, two watches on it. Sign on easel in front of right curtain reads:* MORNING IN THE CITY.

AT RISE: STOREKEEPER, *arms crossed, stands upstage of left table.* WATCHMAKER *stands upstage of right table.* RICH MAN *enters left and crosses to* STOREKEEPER. PEDRO *enters right and crosses to* STOREKEEPER, *careful to stay clear of* RICH MAN, *but paying close attention to what he says and does.*

STOREKEEPER (*To* RICH MAN): *Buenos días, señor.* I have here two wonderful jackets for sale—fine material, latest style.

RICH MAN (*Examining jackets*): Hm-m-m, these are nice jackets. I would look quite handsome wearing either one.

STOREKEEPER: I'm sure you would.

RICH MAN: How much are you asking for them?

STOREKEEPER: Only two hundred *pesos* each.

RICH MAN (*Disgusted*): Two hundred *pesos?* That's way too much.

STOREKEEPER (*Spreading hands*): It is a bargain. These are the best jackets on the market. (*Sighs*) Oh, well, if you buy both, you could have them for one hundred and ninety *pesos* each.

RICH MAN: That's still too much.

STOREKEEPER: Would you have me lose money on these jackets? Come on, *señor.* I am a poor man, and you are a rich man. The price is fair. You can afford both jackets.

RICH MAN: Of course I can afford them, but I'm only interested in the best bargains, and yours aren't good enough. (STOREKEEPER *shrugs, as does* PEDRO.) *Adiós,* Storekeeper. I shall visit the watchmaker instead. (*Crosses to* WATCHMAKER, *followed by* PEDRO, *still careful to stay out of* RICH MAN*'s way.* STOREKEEPER *frowns and crosses arms.*)

WATCHMAKER (*To* RICH MAN): *Buenos días, señor.* I have here two excellent watches. Not only do they keep perfect time, but they are equally stylish.

RICH MAN (*Examining watches*): Hm-m-m, nice watches. Either one would look fine on my wrist.

WATCHMAKER: I'm sure that's true.

RICH MAN: How much are you asking?

WATCHMAKER: Only four hundred *pesos* each.

RICH MAN (*Disgusted*): Four hundred *pesos?* That's way too much.

WATCHMAKER (*Shaking head*): No, it isn't. It's a bargain. These are quality watches. (*Sighs*) Oh, well, if you bought both I could give them to you for three hundred and fifty *pesos* each.

RICH MAN: That's still too much.

WATCHMAKER: It's a fair price. Would you have me lose money on these watches? *Señor,* I'm a poor man; I have to make *some* profit. Surely you, a rich man, can afford to buy both watches.

RICH MAN: Of course I can afford them, but I'm only interested in the best bargains, and yours aren't good enough. (*Sets watches back on table*) *Adiós.* I'm going home to count my money. (*Starts right.* WATCHMAKER *shrugs as does* PEDRO. *Then* WATCHMAKER *crosses arms, sighs.* PEDRO *removes sombrero and hurries over and taps shoulder of* RICH MAN.)

PEDRO: *Señor,* excuse me.

RICH MAN (*Looking at him disdainfully*): You are Pedro, the peasant who used to work for me. (*Angrily*) What do you want now? I have no job for you.

PEDRO: I beg of you, *señor,* let me have a small loan. Lately, my luck has been bad. If you lend me fifty *pesos,* I will pay you back next week with good interest.

RICH MAN: I won't lend you even one *peso.*

PEDRO: Why not?

RICH MAN: In the first place, I don't like people with holes in their *sombreros.* (*Gestures distastefully at* PEDRO's *hat.* PEDRO *frowns.*) In the second place, you don't have anything to offer me, so why should I help you? *Adiós.* (*Exits right in a haughty manner.* STOREKEEPER *and* WATCHMAKER *meet center, shaking heads, looking after* RICH MAN. PEDRO, *studying his hat, crosses to stand between them.*)

STOREKEEPER: That rich man is obnoxious.

WATCHMAKER (*Nodding*): He's always trying to get the best at the expense of others. He only cares about himself.

PEDRO (*Smiling at hat*): I know how we can get the best of him.

STOREKEEPER *and* WATCHMAKER (*In unison*): How?

PEDRO (*Putting on hat*): Listen, *mi amigos*. I have a plan to outwit the rich man, but I'll need your help. Agreed? (*Extends hand, palm up.* STOREKEEPER *and* WATCHMAKER *each slap a hand on his.*)

STOREKEEPER *and* WATCHMAKER (*In unison*): Agreed. (*Blackout.* PEDRO *exits left;* STOREKEEPER *and* WATCHMAKER *return to stand behind tables; new sign on easel reads:* THE NEXT MORNING. *Lights up.*)

RICH MAN (*Sauntering on right, counting money*): Ah, I made a good profit selling my sugar cane. (*Folds up money and puts it in pocket.* PEDRO *enters left and crosses to* STOREKEEPER.)

PEDRO (*Picking up jacket*): How much is this fine jacket?

STOREKEEPER: Only two hundred *pesos*.

PEDRO: That's a bargain. I'll take it. Charge it to my *sombrero.* (*Slips on jacket*)

STOREKEEPER: *Sí*. The jacket is charged to your *sombrero.*

PEDRO: *Gracias.* (RICH MAN *is amazed, blinks, mouth open.* PEDRO *crosses to* WATCHMAKER *and picks up watch.*) How much is this fine watch?

WATCHMAKER: Only four hundred *pesos*.

PEDRO: That's a bargain. I'll take it. Charge it to my *sombrero.* (*Slips on watch*)

WATCHMAKER: *Sí*. The watch is charged to your *sombrero.*

PEDRO: *Gracias.* (RICH MAN *is even more amazed.* PEDRO *starts to pass him to exit right.*)

RICH MAN: Wait a minute. Wait a minute.

PEDRO (*Haughtily*): What do you want?

RICH MAN: Yesterday you said you were down on your luck. You asked me for a loan. Today you are buying a jacket and a watch.

PEDRO: *Sí.*

RICH MAN: How can you do that?

PEDRO: I have discovered that my holey *sombrero* is far more valuable than I realized. It is magical. I can go to any merchant and say, "Charge it to my *sombrero,*" and the merchandise is mine.

RICH MAN: Amazing! What a valuable hat! You must sell it to me.

PEDRO (*Indignantly*): What? Sell it to you? I should say not. Yesterday you wouldn't even lend me a *peso.*

RICH MAN: Forgive me. I must have been out of my mind. Look, I'll give you two hundred *pesos* for your *sombrero.*

PEDRO: No!

RICH MAN: Four hundred *pesos.*

PEDRO (*Louder*): No!

RICH MAN (*Pulling out money*): Six hundred.

PEDRO (*Looking at money*): Well, I don't know.

RICH MAN: Eight hundred. My last offer. Take it or leave it.

PEDRO: I'll take it. You drive a hard bargain. (*Hands him sombrero, takes money, then exits right.* RICH MAN *gleefully rushes over to* WATCHMAKER.)

RICH MAN: I'll buy this watch. (*Picks it up*) Charge it to my *sombrero.*

WATCHMAKER: I can't do that.

RICH MAN: Of course you can. (*Runs to* STORE-KEEPER *and picks up jacket*) Charge this to my *sombrero,* too.

STOREKEEPER: I can't do that.

RICH MAN: Of course you can, of course you can.

WATCHMAKER *and* STOREKEEPER (*In unison*): No, we can't.

RICH MAN (*Sputtering to both*): But, but, you let Pedro charge a jacket and a watch to his *sombrero.* This is the same hat. Why can't I use it the same way?

WATCHMAKER: Because when Pedro owned that *sombrero,* it was the best he had. It was valuable.

STOREKEEPER: Whereas to a rich man, it is only a tattered hat, full of holes, and worth nothing. (RICH MAN *snarls and hurls hat to ground.*)

RICH MAN: I've been tricked. (*Runs off left, shaking fist.*)

WATCHMAKER *and* STOREKEEPER (*Shouting after him in unison*): Adiós, señor. (*Burst into laughter.* PEDRO *reenters, laughs, and counts money.*)

PEDRO (*To* WATCHMAKER): Here are four hundred *pesos* for my watch. (*Hands him money. To* STOREKEEPER) And here are two hundred *pesos* for my jacket. (*Hands him money. Pockets rest of money.*) And two hundred *pesos* for the loan of my holey *sombrero.* (*Puts hat on head. All cheer. Blackout. Curtain*)

THE END

Production Notes

LATINO TRIO

Characters: HORMIGA'S LAWSUIT: traditionally, 8 males; 4 females (however, play can be performed with 12 male or female actors). SEÑORITA CUCARACHA FINDS A HUSBAND: 4 male; 1 female; 1 male or female for Narrator. PEDRO'S HOLEY SOMBRERO: 4 males.

Playing Time: 30 minutes.

Costumes: HORMIGA'S LAWSUIT: Juez wears black robe and carries gavel. Others wear combination of masks, face painting and costumes to indicate their characters; signs on back give names in Spanish and English. Hormiga has two extra legs attached to body, one of them, plus a real leg, wrapped in white sheeting; she carries a crutch. SEÑORITA CUCARACHA FINDS A HUSBAND: Cucaracha wears long, full-skirted dress, has extra set of legs attached to body, long antennae, and carries fan. All have face painting to indicate character. Gato wears dramatic cape. Gallo had red comb on head, red wattle attached to chin and wing-like appendages attached to arms (strips of crepe paper may be used to represent feathers). Sapo is dressed in brown with bumps painted on back. Ratón has large ears and long tail. PEDRO'S HOLEY SOMBRERO: Rich Man wears fancy Spanish clothes. Others wears white shirts and pajama-like pants. Pedro has a sombrero.

Properties: HORMIGA'S LAWSUIT: gavel and crutch. SEÑORITA CUCARACHA FINDS A HUSBAND: fan. PEDRO'S HOLEY SOMBRERO: 2 jackets, 2 watches, fake Mexican money.

Setting: Dark curtain backdrop for all three playlets. HORMIGA'S LAWSUIT: tall podium, tall stool. SEÑORITA CUCARACHA FINDS A HUSBAND: balcony (three-sided, cardboard cutout of railing, painted black to look like wrought iron), small table is right. PEDRO'S HOLEY HAT: two small folding tables, covered with cloths; easel with two signs as indicated in script.

Lighting: Blackouts at times indicated. SEÑORITA CUCARACHA FINDS A HUSBAND: spotlight area where Cucaracha and her suitors pantomime, using soft lights, and add blue flood on upstage area for night atmosphere.

The Talking Burro

The Christmas celebration in Mexico called *Las Posadas* begins on December 16 and lasts through December 24. For nine nights there are processions, people walking through the streets reenacting the search of Mary and Joseph to find a place to stay as they did long ago in Bethlehem.

Usually, a group of children carries a platform that holds Mary and Joseph figures; sometimes instead, especially on the last night, a girl dressed as Mary rides a burro, and a boy dressed as Joseph walks beside her. A child dressed as an angel leads the procession, then come Mary and Joseph, followed by children, then adults, and finally musicians. Carrying *faroles* and singing, chanting, or blowing whistles, the procession travels to different houses, where they beg for shelter but are refused, until finally they are admitted to a house and, after kneeling in prayer, go into the patio for a party.

The same ceremony occurs for eight nights. On the ninth night, Christmas Eve, the ceremony is more elaborate and the procession concludes at a manger scene. The celebration afterwards is very festive, with a *piñata* strung up for the children and food for everybody.

In Southwest portions of the United States where Spain colonized and where Mexico once ruled, especially in towns with a large Hispanic population, the enactment of *Las Posadas* is a Christmas-time tradition, and it is common to see *luminarias,* votive candles in paper bags, lighting porches and walkways.

The Talking Burro

Characters

NARRATOR
BURRO
CARLA
MAMA
PAPA
LA POLICÍA, *the policeman*
EL ALCALDE, *the mayor*
EL MÉDICO, *the doctor*
ROSITA
MANUEL, *her brother*
ABUELA, *their grandmother*
DANCERS, *extras*
SINGERS, *extras*
BOY

SCENE 1

BEFORE RISE: NARRATOR *enters and walks to center.*

NARRATOR: Once upon a time, long ago in the month of Christmas, in the Mexican village of Siqueros there was a very unusual burro. (*He exits. Curtain opens.*)

SETTING: *Early morning in the village of Siqueros. A pile of firewood is center. Backdrop shows cardboard cutouts of houses.*

AT RISE: BURRO *sits center stage, with his head resting on his hands in a "thinker's pose." CARLA enters, carrying bundle of firewood, which she adds to pile, center.*

84

CARLA: Get up, my *burrito*. I have to load this firewood on your back and sell it in the marketplace.

BURRO (*Stubbornly*): No, I don't want to. I am tired of carrying wood.

CARLA (*Astonished*): *Burrito,* you are talking!

BURRO: *Sí, sí,* señorita Carla. Remarkable, isn't it? The words just came out of me.

CARLA: How did you learn to speak like a person?

BURRO: I am not sure. Perhaps it was from listening every day outside the schoolhouse window.

CARLA: Amazing!

BURRO: *Sí,* Señorita. Now, since I am so amazing, I see no reason to carry wood on my back ever again.

CARLA: That is a problem, little burro, for we need your help. (*Suddenly looks offstage*) Here are Mama and Papa. Please be quiet for your own good. (PAPA *and* MAMA *enter. She wears rebozo.*)

PAPA: Carla, why isn't the burro ready to go to market?

CARLA: Well, ah, Papa, I, ah—

BURRO (*Interrupting, singing*): "*La cucaracha, la cucaracha . . .*"

MAMA (*Startled, looking about*): Who is singing?

CARLA (*Aside, to* BURRO): Sh-h-h, hush. (BURRO, *ignoring her, grabs* MAMA'*s rebozo in teeth and pulls it away from her. Then he flips it around his shoulders, stands on hind legs, with one hoof on hip and other over head, and begins stamping out a flamenco dance.*)

MAMA (*Yelling*): Give back my *rebozo!*

BURRO (*With a sigh*): All right. (*Tosses rebozo to her*) I was just having a little fun. Where's your sense of humor?

MAMA *and* PAPA (*Shocked*): ¡*Caramba!* The burro speaks!

PAPA: He has gone *loco.* I'd better get the police. (*Running right and left; shouting*) ¡*Policía!* ¡*Policía!*

MAMA: I think the mayor should know about this. (*Exits left, shouting*) ¡*El alcalde, el alcalde!*

PAPA: Maybe I should get the doctor, too. (*Exits right; shouting*) *¡El médico, el médico!*

CARLA: Little burro, see what you have done?

BURRO: But I am happy with my beautiful new voice. I cannot keep still. Suddenly, I feel free. (*Leaps in ballet fashion*)

CARLA: There is no telling what will happen to you now. *La policía* may put you in jail. (BURRO *groans.*)

BURRO: That all sounds frightful. I must leave town— *pronto.* It will be good to get away from working. I will explore the world and have a marvelous time. (*Waving a hoof*) *Adiós,* Carla.

CARLA (*Waving sadly*): *Adiós, burrito.* (BURRO *exits right.* LA POLICÍA *enters left, running, with cap gun. He fires caps.* CARLA *hides behind house in fright.*)

LA POLICÍA: Where is the outlaw burro? (*Prowls around stage with gun ready.* EL ALCALDE *enters left, napkin tucked under chin.* LA POLICÍA *whirls about and pokes him with gun.* EL ALCALDE *shrieks and jumps.* LA POLICÍA *is embarrassed.*)

EL ALCALDE: *¡Cuidado!* Be careful! Where is the creature that interrupted my breakfast? As mayor of this town, I declare him unconstitutional. (EL MÉDICO *enters right, carrying doctor's bag and tongue depressor.*)

EL MÉDICO: *Buenos días,* Señor Policía and Señor Alcalde. Where is this sick burro? I shall examine his throat. I can tell by the color of his tongue what his sickness is. What color is his tongue? Do you know?

LA POLICÍA *and* EL ALCALDE (*Shrugging, ad lib*): I'm not sure. I don't know. (*Etc.*)

EL MÉDICO, LA POLICÍA *and* EL ALCALDE (*Looking about; together*): Where is that crazy burro? (PAPA *and* MAMA *enter, looking around cautiously.*)

PAPA (*To* MAMA): The burro was here a moment ago! What is wrong? (CARLA *comes out from behind house, and comes downstage.*)

CARLA: *Buenos días,* Mama and Papa. You are looking for the burro, I see.

EL MÉDICO (*To* PAPA, MAMA, *and* CARLA): I believe your burro has an extremely rare disease, so rare, actually, that it may not yet have been discovered. (*Exits*)

LA POLICÍA (*Tucking gun in belt*): If I find the burro, I will put hoof cuffs on it. (*Exits*)

EL ALCALDE: Excuse me. My beans are getting cold, and I like my *frijoles* hot. (*Exits*)

MAMA: *Adiós,* Señor Alcalde.

CARLA (*To* PAPA): The burro has run away.

PAPA (*Dejectedly*): Now we will have to carry all of the firewood on our own backs. (PAPA, MAMA, *and* CARLA *exit, heads lowered, each carrying wood. Curtain*)

* * * * *

SCENE 2

BEFORE RISE: NARRATOR *enters and walks to center.*

NARRATOR: For three days, the burro walked across the desert. For three nights, he shivered in the cold wind. He decided that exploring the world was not a good idea for him. He grew more and more tired, hungry, thirsty, and lonely. Then on the fourth day, he arrived at a beautiful town with trees and flowers. It was Mazatlán. (*Curtain opens*)

* * *

SETTING: *Mexican village of Mazatlán. Houses used in Scene 1 are rearranged against backdrop. There are potted trees near houses, and paper flowers surround a cardboard cutout of a fountain, center.*

AT RISE: ROSITA *pantomimes filling her olla with water*

from the fountain. BURRO *staggers on stage.* ROSITA *notices him.*

ROSITA: Poor *burrito,* come have a drink at the fountain.

BURRO: *Muchas gracias,* señorita. Thank you very much. (*Pantomimes drinking*)

ROSITA (*Astonished*): You speak! How amazing to meet a talking animal.

BURRO (*Fearfully*): You won't put me in jail, or throw me in the river, or haul me off to the hospital, will you?

ROSITA (*Laughing*): Of course not, little burro.

ABUELA (*Calling from offstage*): *Tortillas* for sale. *Tortillas* for sale. (*Enters with basket of tortillas*)

ROSITA: Here is my grandmother.

ABUELA: *Buenas tardes,* Rosita.

ROSITA: Good afternoon to you, too, Abuela. We have a special burro here. He speaks with a human voice.

ABUELA (*Sizing up* BURRO): Hm-m-m, how interesting! He might do. He *will* do. Yes, this burro will be the one.

BURRO (*Suspiciously*): The one for *what?*

ABUELA (*Laughing*): For *Las Posadas.* (*Calls offstage*) Manuel, come here. (*To* ROSITA) Isn't it true that your brother, Manuel, is going to be José, in the Christmas pageant?

ROSITA (*Smiling*): *Sí,* and I am honored to play the holy mother, Maria.

MANUEL (*Entering*): What is it, Abuela?

ABUELA: We have found a talking burro to carry Maria in *Las Posadas.* A special burro for a special job.

MANUEL (*Surprised*): *¡Caramba!* A talking burro! I don't believe it!

BURRO: Tell me more about this Christmas pageant.

MANUEL (*To* BURRO): In this pageant, we pretend

our town of Mazatlán is Bethlehem. Each night we go to a different house, asking for a place to rest.

ROSITA: The people in each house say, "No, there is no room here. *No hay posada.*"

MANUEL: For eight nights we knock on doors, asking for a resting place, but each night there is *no hay posada.*

ROSITA: Finally, on the ninth night, the landlord of one house says, "*Sí*, you may stay here."

ABUELA (*Proudly*): And this year, I shall play the landlord in the pageant. I let José and María into the house and we pretend that is the place *el niño*, the baby, is born.

BURRO (*Pleased*): I like that idea.

ABUELA: It is settled then. Burro, you will carry Rosita in *Las Posadas. Adiós.* (*Exits, calling*) *Tortillas* for sale.

ROSITA (*To* BURRO): Little burro, eat well tonight, and have a good rest, for tomorrow is a big day— tomorrow the Christmas *fiesta* begins! (*Curtain*)

* * * * *

SCENE 3

BEFORE RISE: NARRATOR *enters and walks to center.*

NARRATOR: Back in the village of Siqueros, Carla, Mama, and Papa were getting ready for Christmas. But they were sad, for they missed their burro. (*Curtain opens.*)

* * *

TIME: *The morning of the festival of Las Posadas.*

SETTING: *Same as Scene 1. Traditional tools for grinding corn (mano and metate) are at center.*

AT RISE: MAMA *and* CARLA *are taking turns grinding corn.* PAPA *sits nearby, painting wooden toy.*

PAPA (*Shaking head sadly*): I wish our little burro were here to take us to Mazatlán for the Christmas celebration.

MAMA (*Wistfully*): I wish our little burro were here to carry firewood to the market place.

CARLA (*Tearfully*): I wish *burrito* were here because he is *mi amigo,* my friend.

PAPA (*Rising*): Enough sadness. (*Holds up toy*) Look, my last toy is finished. It is going to be one of the many presents to fall out of the big *piñata* at *Las Posadas* in Mazatlán. How do you like it, Carla?

CARLA: It is a beautiful toy, Papa.

PAPA: I am sorry we cannot go to Mazatlán this year and deliver the toy personally. If only our burro had not run away.

EL ALCALDE (*Entering*): *Buenos días.* I have good news for you.

CARLA (*Jumping up; excitedly*): Señor Alcalde, has our burro been found?

EL ALCALDE: No, no. Señor Médico, and Señor Policía and I are going to Mazatlán. There is room in our cart for the three of you, if you would like to go. (MAMA *and* PAPA *jump up in excitement.*)

CARLA, MAMA, *and* PAPA (*Ad lib; happily*): *Sí, sí!* How wonderful! (*Etc.*)

EL ALCALDE: Then, get ready. The oxen are being hitched to the *carreta* now. (*Exits*)

CARLA, MAMA, *and* PAPA (*Ad lib*): We are going to Mazatlán! I am so happy! (*Etc. They pick up mano, metate, and corn, and exit. Curtain*)

* * * * *

SCENE 4

BEFORE RISE: NARRATOR *enters and walks to center.*

NARRATOR: In Mexico, *Las Posadas* is the way of celebrating Christmas. On the ninth night of the celebration, which is Christmas Eve, María and José look for their resting place, and at last find it. Everybody is happy and celebrates with singing, dancing, games, and feasting. It is said by all who were in Mazatlán that on Christmas, the burro carried María with great dignity. There were a few people who claimed they heard the burro's voice, joining in the singing, and that the sound was that of an angel.

* * *

TIME: *The night of Las Posadas.*

SETTING: *Same as Scene 2, except for rope, which hangs center.*

AT RISE: SINGERS *are kneeling around fountain, holding lighted candles (or small flashlights). SINGERS sing, or chant to guitar chords, the following traditional song of Las Posadas, an appeal for shelter. They may sing in English, in Spanish, which follows each verse, or in both. As SINGERS begin song, pantomime characters* MANUEL *and* ABUELA, *dressed as José and Landlord enter, followed by* ROSITA, *as María, who walks beside* BURRO, *as if riding. A pantomime scene accompanies song.*

SINGERS:
In the name of heaven,
Kind landlord,
Please give these pilgrims
Shelter tonight.

En nombre del cielo,
Buen propietario,
Por favor deles a estos peregrinos
Posada para esta noche.

(MANUEL *pantomimes knocking on door, while* ROSITA *stands near him with* BURRO.)

There is no room.
Try another house.
Go away quickly.
You waste my time.

No hay posada.
Busquen otra casa.
Váyanse rápido.
Me roban el tiempo.

(ABUELA *pantomimes opening door, and shakes head.*)

But I am Joseph.
My wife is Mary.
Please give these pilgrims
Shelter tonight.

Pero yo soy José.
Mi esposa es María.
Por favor deles a estos peregrinos
Posada para esta noche.

(MANUEL *points to* ROSITA, *and then holds out his hands, clasped, to* ABUELA *as though begging.*)

I did not recognize you.
Forgive me, Joseph and Mary.
Enter, good travelers.
You are welcome in this house.

No les reconocía.
Discúlpen, José y María.
Adelante, buenos viajeros.
Están ustedes en su casa.

(ABUELA *throws arms open wide, pantomimes opening door, and gestures for* MANUEL *and* ROSITA *to enter.* Then, MANUEL, ROSITA, ABUELA, *and* BURRO *exit.* SINGERS *blow out candles, or turn off flashlights, then exit right, humming song.* BURRO *reenters left, wearing garland of flowers.* PAPA, MAMA, *and* CARLA *reenter right, unseen by* BURRO.)

MAMA: Look, there is the burro that carried María in the pageant.

PAPA: That burro looks familiar.

CARLA: *Sí.* I wonder why the burro seems so sad?

ABUELA (*Entering, crossing to* BURRO): You did well, *burrito.* Where will you go now?

BURRO (*Sadly*): I have no place to go.

CARLA (*Hearing* BURRO; *excitedly*): The burro talked! It is our burro. (*Runs to hug him*) *Burrito,* at last we have found you.

BURRO (*Gleefully*): Carla! Mama! Papa! How wonderful to see you!

PAPA (*Crossing to* BURRO *with* MAMA; *proudly*): Our burro was in *Las Posadas.* (*To* BURRO) You make us very proud.

MAMA: But we miss you.

CARLA: Very much.

BURRO: I miss all of you, too. I find I am only happy when I can be useful. May I come home with you?

PAPA: Of course. And, from now on, *burrito,* we will share the loads with you. You will not carry everything yourself.

MAMA: *Sí.* You should have some time each day to kick up your hooves.

BURRO (*Kicking up hooves*): *Muchas gracias, amigos.* Thank you, friends. (LA POLICÍA *enters, firing cap gun.* ABUELA, MAMA, PAPA, *and* CARLA *scream and hide behind fountain.* BURRO *remains in place.*)

LA POLICÍA (*Pointing gun at* BURRO): Are you the outlaw, talking burro? (BURRO *places hoof over mouth and shakes head.* EL ALCALDE *enters with napkin under chin, carrying a tortilla with frijoles.*)

EL ALCALDE: Why does everything happen when I am eating my *frijoles?* (EL MÉDICO *enters, carrying doctor's bag and tongue depressor, and crosses to* BURRO.)

EL MÉDICO (*To* BURRO): Open your mouth and say "hee haw." (BURRO *backs away, frightened.*)

CARLA (*Running out from behind fountain to* BURRO; *to* EL MÉDICO): There is nothing wrong with our burro. (*To* BURRO) Isn't that right, my *burrito?* (BURRO *starts to answer, but can't seem to speak.*)

BURRO (*Screeching*): Hee haw!

MAMA (*Coming out from behind fountain; to* BURRO): What did you say?

BURRO: Hee haw, hee haw.

PAPA (*Coming out from behind fountain with* ABUELA): I think he has lost his human voice.

BURRO (*Nodding*): Heee hawww! (*All laugh.*)

LA POLICÍA (*Tucking gun in belt*): Amigos, this is only an ordinary burro. (*Exits*)

EL ALCALDE: Back to my *frijoles.* At last, I can eat in peace. (*Exits*)

EL MÉDICO (*Examining* BURRO): An extremely healthy animal. He does not even have fleas. (*Exits*)

ABUELA (*To* CARLA): It may be your burro was given a voice only for Christmas. (*In wonder*) Perhaps it was a miracle.

CARLA (*Slowly*): You may be right, Abuela.

PAPA: Tonight we shall take our burro home.

MAMA: But before we go, there is still time to dance and sing. (DANCERS, SINGERS, *and* BOY *enter, shouting.*)

DANCERS *and* SINGERS (*Ad lib; together*): Bravo! It's time to celebrate! (*Etc.* DANCERS *perform dance with* BURRO, *while everyone claps and sings. During dance,* PAPA *exits and returns with piñata, stick, and blindfold. He hangs piñata from rope, center. The dance ends, and everyone ad libs excitedly.*)

ALL (*Ad lib*): Ah, the *piñata*. Let the youngest boy hit it first. I want my turn. (*Etc.* PAPA *goes to* BOY *on stage, blindfolds him and hands him stick. He spins him around several times, then releases him.*)

PAPA (*To* BOY): There you go. Now try to hit the *piñata*. (BOY *takes a few steps, then raises stick to try to hit piñata.*)

ALL (*Ad lib*): You can do it! To the right! No, to the left! (*Etc. As curtain starts to close slowly, the* NARRATOR *walks on. After curtain is closed, he begins to speak.*)

NARRATOR: The villagers celebrated Christmas in this way every year. As for the burro, he proved to be a hard worker. He shared the loads with Papa and only rested when Carla took him out to play—then, he kicked up his hooves. Because the burro was such a hard worker, El Alcalde appointed him the official mascot of the village of Siqueros. Carla, Papa, and Mama were proud of him, and the burro was very happy. (*Curtain*)

THE END

Production Notes

THE TALKING BURRO

Characters: 3 male; 4 female; 5 male or female for Burro, Narrator, El Alcalde, El Médico, La Policía; as many male and female dancers and singers as desired.

Playing Time: 25 to 30 minutes, depending on time spent dancing and singing.

Costumes: Traditional Mexican peasant dress. El Médico wears white, high-collared smock. La Policía, vest, police hat, boots, and badge. El Alcalde, black sombrero, pants, short jacket with gold braid, napkin tucked into shirt collar, and string tie. Papa, Manuel, and male dancers and singers wear serapes or ponchos, sombreros, sashes, and sandals or boots. Female singers and dancers, full long skirts, peasant-style blouses, sashes, *rebozos* (scarves) worn on shoulders or covering head, sandals, and at festival, jewelry and flowers in hair. Abuela, black dress and *rebozo* worn on head. Burro, *papier-mâché* head, gray shirt and pants, yarn tail and cardboard hooves attached to ankles and wrists.

Properties: Firewood; cap pistol with caps; doctor's bag; large tongue depressor; small wooden toy; paint brush; candles (or small flashlights); *olla* (earthenware crock); basket of tortillas; ears of corn; cornmeal; mano and metate; piñata; blindfold; stick.

Setting: Villages of Siqueros and Mazatlán, with cardboard cut-outs of flat-roofed adobe houses. In Scene 1, there is a pile of firewood at center. In Scenes 2, 3, and 4, there are potted trees, paper flowers, and a fountain at center. In Scene 4, a rope also hangs center for piñata.

Sound: Record or live guitar music to accompany singing and dancing.

Lighting: In Scene 4, if singers with candles are on stage instead of in a processional, stage is dark until candles are blown out, and then lights go up.

A Gift for Pachacuti Inca

Long before the establishment of the Inca Empire, other great civilizations existed in Peru, mainly on the coastal deserts. In fact, carbon 14 testing indicates man was there as far back as 3000 B.C.

In the early 11th century A.D., in the valley of Cuzco in the Andes Mountains, lived a people called the Quechuas (speakers of Quechua, a language still spoken in the Andes). These people were ruled by kings called Incas. The name Inca is popularly used today to refer to the entire culture. In some ways the Incas can be compared to the Romans: They were adept in creating a road system, keeping records, conquering and ruling other tribes, and assimilating the traditions and techniques of other cultures. Above all, the Incas were organizers.

The Inca, the ruler, was considered divine, a descendant of the Sun, believed to be the creator of everything. He was all powerful and exacted tributes from his people. Pachacuti Inca was the ninth king, crowned in 1433, about a hundred years before the Spanish conquest of the region.

The descendants of the indigenous people who live in the Andes and work as farmers are today referred to as *campesinos*. They have retained much of their old lifestyle, intermingled with Spanish-brought Catholicism. As in many Latin American countries, great social and economic barriers exist between indigenous people and those of Spanish descent.

A Gift for Pachacuti Inca

Characters

CHIMU
SUMAC, *his wife*
MACANA, *his lazy brother*
CATU, *Macana's wife*
RECORDER
CHIEF
LLAMA
THREE VILLAGERS
CROWD OF VILLAGERS
MOUNTAIN ⎤
CANYON   ⎬ *Spirits*
PUNA   ⎦

SCENE 1

TIME: *Long ago.*
SETTING: *Ancient Inca village or ayllu in what is today Peru. Backdrop shows Andes Mountains. There is a folding screen at right, representing Chimu's house. Folded length of striped fabric is in front of screen. String of dried corn and chili peppers hangs from screen. Stool is at center.*
AT RISE: *Appropriate South American flute music is heard. Music fades as 1ST VILLAGER runs on, waving arms.*

1ST VILLAGER (*Shouting*): News, everyone! News! (VILLAGERS, CHIMU, SUMAC, MACANA *and* CATU *enter from opposite sides of stage.* MACANA *and* CATU *stand apart from others.*)

98

VILLAGERS (*Ad lib*): What is the news? Is the chief coming? Hurry! (*Etc.*)

1ST VILLAGER: A courier brings word to our village that Pachacuti Inca, the new king, has been crowned! (*All cheer.*)

2ND VILLAGER: Does that mean that the chief will collect our gifts soon?

1ST VILLAGER: Yes—the chief arrives today. Each one of us must present his gift for the new Inca. It is forbidden to disobey.

3RD VILLAGER: May the giant condor protect me! I must finish my carving at once. (*Runs off*)

2ND VILLAGER (*Turning and starting off*): I am making an incense burner—it is nearly done. (*Exits*)

VILLAGERS (*Ad lib; starting to exit*): What is your gift? Have you dyed your wool? (*Etc.* VILLAGERS *exit, followed by* MACANA *and* CATU.)

CHIMU: Sumac, my wife, is your gift for the new king ready?

SUMAC (*Crossing to their house*): The cloth I have woven is finished, Chimu. (*Holds up cloth for him to see*)

CHIMU: Good! (*He examines cloth proudly.*) It has taken you two months to weave this fine material. I am very proud of your work.

SUMAC (*With a slight bow*): Thank you, husband. Although I have spent long hours at my loom, my heart is happy now for the result is a pleasure to you. Do you think Pachacuti Inca will like this?

CHIMU (*Unfolding cloth*): Excellent! It is excellent! He is certain to admire its quality. (SUMAC *carefully folds cloth, and she and* CHIMU *sit down in front of screen. Meanwhile,* MACANA *and* CATU *enter.*)

MACANA (*Angrily*): Catu, it's your fault we have nothing to give.

CATU: *My* fault! Macana, why do you always blame me?

MACANA: Because you are the laziest wife north of Cuzco.

CATU: Hah! Did *you* make anything for the king? No! Not even a small piece of pottery. You spent your time snoring like an earthquake, shaking the walls. Some morning I'll wake up under a heap of fallen stone, if indeed I wake up at all.

MACANA (*Taunting*): You'd rather sleep than work, anyway.

CATU (*Angrily*): What? (MACANA *sees* CHIMU *and* SUMAC. *He gestures for* CATU *to be quiet. He points toward* CHIMU *and* SUMAC.)

MACANA: Sh-h! Catu, do you see my brother there?

CATU: Of course I do. Chimu is a fine man. He works five times harder in the potato field than you do.

MACANA: How I dislike my brother! Everyone is always saying, "Chimu works hard." "Chimu is a good man." Chimu is this—Chimu is that—I am nothing when Chimu is around.

CATU: Without a gift for the new king, we may *both* become nothing.

MACANA: I know! (*Looks again at* CHIMU) Wife, I have an idea that I believe will solve our problem. (*Crosses to* CHIMU. CATU *follows*.) Good day, dear brother.

CHIMU: Macana, welcome to you and your wife.

MACANA (*Touching cloth*): This is beautiful weaving.

CHIMU: It is our present for the new king.

MACANA (*Sighing sadly*): You are lucky people to be able to give such a gift. (*Sniffs and begins to sob. Aside to* CATU) Start crying, Catu. (CATU *looks puzzled, then starts wailing.*)

SUMAC: What is wrong? Are you both ill?

CHIMU: Brother, why do you cry so?

MACANA: Alas! We *had* such a magnificent gift for Pachacuti Inca.

CHIMU: What happened?

MACANA: Oh-h-h! A giant condor swooped out of the sky and flew away with it. Is that not so, wife?

CATU: Ay-y-y! It is so.

CHIMU: What was your gift?

MACANA (*Hesitating*): A—kind of pot.

CATU: Ay-yi-yi, a *large* pot.

SUMAC: I did not know you made pottery, Macana.

CATU: Oh, yes. He works secretly at night. (MACANA *nods, pretending to wipe away tears.*)

CHIMU (*Patting* MACANA's *shoulder*): I'm sorry, brother. It must make you sad to have your gift stolen. But surely there is something else you can give.

MACANA: No, there is nothing. I have nothing to give Pachacuti Inca. It will mean certain death for us. (CATU *wails again.*)

SUMAC: My husband, we cannot let your brother and his wife suffer such an end.

CHIMU: But, what can we do?

SUMAC: Could we not say my cloth was partly woven by Catu?

CHIMU (*Thoughtfully looking at cloth*): It is a perfect piece, and it took you a long time to weave. Yes, it could easily be the work of two weavers.

SUMAC: It is settled then. (*To* MACANA *and* CATU) Do not cry any more. When the chief of our province arrives, both our families will present this gift.

CATU *and* MACANA (*Bowing and clasping hands*): Thank you. Oh, thank you.

MACANA (*Slyly*): Why not let us keep the cloth until it is time to present it?

CHIMU: Well, I suppose . . .

MACANA (*Interrupting*): Catu and I would like to examine your fine work. (*Taking cloth*) How kind you both are. Oh, Chimu, I am so glad I have you for a brother. (*Lights dim and flute plays to indicate passage of time.* CHIMU, CATU, MACANA, *and* SUMAC *exit. As lights come up, flute music ceases, and* RECORDER *enters, carrying knotted string or "quipu."*)

RECORDER (*Calling*): Ayllu! Ayllu! The chief is arriving. Bring forth your gifts. (CHIEF *enters, walking proudly, and sits on stool.* VILLAGERS *enter, each carrying gift.* CHIMU, SUMAC, MACANA *and* CATU *enter last.* MACANA *carries cloth.*) Let the gifts for Pachacuti Inca be presented to the chief. (VILLAGERS *file up to* CHIEF, *kneel and present gifts, which* CHIEF *examines. Then* VILLAGERS *kneel at right and left of* CHIEF. RECORDER *ties knots in quipu as each gift is recorded. Flute music plays throughout. After* VILLAGERS *have presented gifts,* MACANA *and* CHIMU *start toward* CHIEF. VILLAGERS *watch. Suddenly,* MACANA *stops, puts out hand and stops* CHIMU.)

MACANA: Stay here, Chimu. *I* will present the gift.

CHIMU: But, we should both—

MACANA (*Interrupting*): I said, stay here! Come, Catu. (MACANA *and* CATU *go forward, kneeling to one side of* CHIEF. MACANA *holds out cloth.*) O great Chief, I am Macana, and this is my wife, Catu. To Pachacuti Inca we present this cloth, which my wife has spent many months weaving.

CHIEF (*Feeling material*): This is the finest material I have seen in my province.

CHIMU (*Rushing forward*): Wait! Wait!

CHIEF: Who is this man?

CHIMU: I am Chimu. It was *my* wife, Sumac, who wove that cloth.

MACANA: Pay no attention to him. That lazy man does not have a gift. Why, only this morning, he begged me to say this cloth came from his family, too. (SUMAC *gasps and runs to* CHIMU's *side.* VILLAGERS *look at each other in surprise, some shrugging, others shaking their heads in disbelief.*)

CHIEF: Disgraceful!

CHIMU: It is not true! Macana, you came to *us*. You begged to share *our* gift, because you had none of your own.

MACANA: I fear the sun has affected this man's head. He is trying to excuse his laziness.

CHIMU: You are my brother, and you—

MACANA (*Interrupting with a laugh*): Do you see how strangely he acts?

CHIEF: Chimu, our empire has little patience with a man who does not work hard. Go and search in the mountains until the sun's rays strike the peaks of the Andes. If you cannot find a suitable gift for the king by sunset, you and your wife will be thrown from the steepest cliff into the Urubamba River. (VILLAGERS *gasp in horror.*)

CHIMU: But, this cloth—

CHIEF (*Interrupting*): Chimu, find your *own* gift for Pachacuti Inca. (MACANA *and* CATU *exchange sly smiles.*)

MACANA (*With mock concern*): Oh, Chimu, I'm sorry that you have no gift. It must make you sad.

CATU: Yes. What a pity you were so lazy! (CHIMU *and* SUMAC *look at each other, bewildered.*)

CHIEF (*Rising and shouting*): Go! Go! You are wasting my time! (CHIMU *slowly exits right. Curtain.*)

* * * * *

SCENE 2

SETTING: *Plateau in high Andes Mountains. Screen, at right, covered with black cloth, represents cave. Downstage there is a black cooking pot on fire of logs. At center is a rock.*

AT RISE: MOUNTAIN, CANYON *and* PUNA, *spirits of the Andes, sit around fire.* LLAMA *is grazing at center.* CHIMU *enters right, walking slowly and wearily to center.*

CHIMU: I have searched the mountains until my bones are numb with cold. I have seen plants and stones and a few grazing llamas, but nothing I could give to the new king. (*Looking around*) Soon it will be sunset.

LLAMA: Hello, Chimu. I've been waiting for you. (CHIMU, *startled, looks around.*)

CHIMU: Who speaks? It is strange. I see no one here.

LLAMA: I—the llama—am speaking!

CHIMU (*Amazed*): A llama who speaks? Perhaps Macana is right about the sun affecting my head.

LLAMA: Nonsense! Listen to me. The sun is setting, and you must go back to your village soon with a gift for the king. Do you see this stone? (*Points to stone with hoof*)

CHIMU: I see it.

LLAMA: Take it to that cave. (*Nods head toward cave, right.*) You will find three spirits waiting for you. They will tell you what to do with the stone.

CHIMU: I don't understand, but I will do as you say. (*Picks up stone and crosses to cave.*)

MOUNTAIN (*Rising*): I am the Spirit of the Andes Mountains.

CANYON: I am the Spirit of the Steep Canyons.

PUNA: I am the Spirit of the High, Flat Puna.

CANYON: For many suns, we have watched you and your wife work.

PUNA: We want to reward you both for your hard labors.

MOUNTAIN: I am grateful for the way you have terraced your mountain fields and made a wall of stone to keep the soil on my sides.

CHIMU: I am grateful to have your soul, Spirit of the Mountain. It feeds my family. But now I am in danger. If I cannot find a gift for Pachacuti Inca, my wife and I will perish.

MOUNTAIN: Then let me help you as you have helped

me in the past. Place the rock into the black pot. (CHIMU *places rock in pot. Spirits wave hands over pot.*)

SPIRITS (*Chanting*):
Chila, chila, cho, cho.
Tacca, tacca, teeco.

CANYON: Reach into the pot, Chimu, and bring out what you find there. (CHIMU *hesitates.*)

PUNA: Don't be afraid, Chimu. We would not hurt you. (CHIMU *reaches into pot and brings out gold llama statue.*)

CHIMU (*Astonished*): It is a statue of a llama. (*Looking closely at statue*) It appears to be made of gold!

SPIRITS: It *is* made of gold!

CHIMU: I can't believe such good fortune!

MOUNTAIN: Now, you have a gift for Pachacuti Inca. (*Looking at sky*) It is almost time for the sun to set. Hurry back to your village, Chimu. (*Sits*)

CHIMU: You have saved me and my wife as well. I am most grateful. (CHIMU *bows. Spirits nod.* CHIMU *crosses right and speaks to* LLAMA.) This golden statue will save my life, friend llama. Thank you for your help.

LLAMA: We shall meet again, Chimu, sooner than you realize. (CHIMU *exits. Curtain.*)

* * * * *

SCENE 3

TIME: *Sunset.*

SETTING: *Same as Scene 1.*

AT RISE: CHIEF *sits on stool, center, with* RECORDER *standing beside him.* MACANA *and* CATU *stand near* CHIEF, *whispering to each other and smiling wickedly.* SU-MAC *stands down right, looking offstage for* CHIMU. VILLAGERS *stand upstage, looking off right and at the sky.*

1ST VILLAGER: The sun is low in the sky.

2ND VILLAGER: I fear Chimu will not find a gift in time.

SUMAC (*Suddenly pointing off right; excitedly*): Look! It is Chimu! He has returned! (CHIMU *hurries in, carrying llama statue. He pats* SUMAC's *arm, reassuringly.* VILLAGERS *move forward curiously.* CHIEF, MACANA *and* CATU *watch.*)

VILLAGERS (*Ad lib*): Ah! He comes. I was afraid he would not make it. What will happen now? (*Etc.*)

1ST VILLAGER: He has something in his hand.

2ND VILLAGER: It shines. What is it? (CHIMU *crosses to* CHIEF *and kneels before him.*)

CHIMU: I have found a gift for Pachacuti Inca. (*Holds out statue.* CHIEF *takes it, examining it closely.*)

VILLAGERS (*In admiration*): Ah-h-h!

1ST VILLAGER: What a beautiful statue!

2ND VILLAGER: A llama of gold!

CHIEF: Where did you find this?

CHIMU: High in the Andes, I met a llama who could talk. He gave me a stone and sent me to the cave of three spirits. When I placed the stone in their magical cooking pot, it turned into this golden statue.

MACANA (*To* CHIEF): Do not believe him. (*To* CHIMU) Come now, Chimu. Do you think you can get away with this? From what wealthy man did you steal the statue?

CHIMU: I speak the truth.

MACANA (*Angrily*): You lie! (*To* CHIEF) I will go to this cave myself. If what Chimu says is true, then we will put more stones into this magical pot and have many more golden gifts for Pachacuti Inca. If it is not true, then this man (*Pointing to* CHIMU) is a thief and should be punished.

CHIEF: We will go to the cave and find out who speaks the truth.

1ST VILLAGER (*To other* VILLAGERS): Let us *all* go.

VILLAGERS (*Nodding, ad lib*): Yes, yes! We should go. Of course. (*Etc.*)

CHIEF: Lead the way, Chimu. (CHIMU *exits right, followed by* CHIEF. SUMAC, MACANA, CATU *and* VILLAGERS *follow them off as curtains close.*)

* * * * *

SCENE 4

SETTING: *The same as Scene 2.*

AT RISE: MOUNTAIN, CANYON, *and* PUNA *are sitting around fire.* LLAMA *is grazing at center.* CHIMU *enters, followed by* CHIEF, SUMAC, MACANA, CATU, *and* VILLAGERS.)

CHIMU (*To* CHIEF): This is the llama—the same llama I met before.

LLAMA (*Pointing to stone with hoof*): This is the stone— the same stone you saw before.

1ST VILLAGER: Look! There is the llama. He speaks!

2ND VILLAGER: Amazing!

1ST VILLAGER: There are the spirits at the caves, just as Chimu said. (MACANA *looks surprised. Suddenly he picks up stone and crosses to cave.*)

MACANA (*Arrogantly*): We shall see if this stone turns to gold for me. (*Pushes Spirits aside rudely and drops stone into pot.* LLAMA *exits behind cave. Spirits wave arms over pot.*)

SPIRITS (*Chanting*):

Tacca, tacca, teeco.

Chila, chila, cho, cho.

(*Deep rumbling sound is heard. It grows louder. Spirits rise dramatically with uplifted arms.* VILLAGERS *scream in terror.*)

1ST VILLAGER (*Shouting*): The ground is shaking!

2ND VILLAGER (*Shouting*): It is an earthquake!

VILLAGERS (*Falling to knees, shrieking; ad lib*): Earthquake! Help! Help! (*Etc. MACANA tries to run away, but falls, center. CATU runs to him and both cower in fear. SUMAC runs to CHIMU. Rumble grows softer.*)

MOUNTAIN (*Calling*): Macana! (*Points to cooking pot on fire*) Is *this* the pot the giant condor swooped out of the sky and stole away from you? (*CANYON and PUNA cackle. MACANA groans and hides his face in hands.*)

CANYON: Speak again, great Spirit of the Andes Mountains. Speak again. (*Louder rumbling. VILLAGERS moan in terror.*)

PUNA (*Shouting*): Tell the people the truth. (*Rumbling ends with a loud crash. All freeze.*)

MOUNTAIN: Macana! Catu! Did you weave the cloth which you gave to the Pachacuti Inca?

MACANA *and* CATU (*Trembling with fear*): No.

CATU: Sumac, Chimu's wife, wove the cloth.

MOUNTAIN (*In deep tones*): Chimu and his wife are honest and they have always worked hard. Macana and his wife are cruel and dishonest. They are the ones who should be punished. I shall take them with me, to a high mountain peak. (*MACANA and CATU draw back in fear.*) There I shall turn them into two sharp stones. For all time, they shall face the howling winter winds. (*Drum beat is heard from offstage.*)

MACANA *and* CATU (*Crying out*): No! No! (*MOUNTAIN crosses right majestically, with arms folded, and exits, while VILLAGERS shrink away. As if in a trance, MACANA and CATU rise and exit right, followed by CANYON and PUNA. Drum stops. VILLAGERS rise and turn to right, staring into distance with wonder.*)

VILLAGERS (*Suddenly pointing*): Look! Look!

1ST VILLAGER: Two rocks are growing on the mountain peaks.

2ND VILLAGER (*Pointing off right*): They are Macana and Catu!

CHIEF: The Spirit of the Mountain has turned them into stone. What he said was true. (CHIEF *turns to* CHIMU *and* SUMAC, *who kneel before him. He takes them by the hands and raises them up.*) Chimu—Sumac—I have misjudged you. Your brother Macana deceived me with his lies. But now I see that you have given the finest gifts of all to Pachacuti Inca! (VILLAGERS *cheer. Flute music is heard from offstage.* VILLAGERS *run to* CHIMU *and* SUMAC *to congratulate them, then begin a folk dance as curtains close.*)

THE END

Production Notes

A GIFT FOR PACHACUTI INCA

Characters: 4 male; 2 female; 4 male or female for Llama and Spirits; as many extras as desired for Villagers.

Playing Time: 20 minutes.

Costumes: Traditional Inca dress. Chief wears hat with medallion on front. Llama wears animal costume (cotton may be attached to shirt and tights; head made of paper-mâché). Spirits wear robes: white for Mountain, gray for Puna, black for Canyon. Each spirit has hat with cardboard cutout representing his character.

Properties: Striped fabric, gifts for new king (pottery, weaving, statues, boxes, etc.), rock, gold llama statue (clay or papier-mâché), quipu (yarn and string).

Setting: Ancient Inca village or *ayllu* in what is today Peru. There is a backdrop painting of snow-capped mountains with terraced fields, roads, and swinging bridges across steep canyons. Scenes 1 and 3: Folding screen at right represents Chimu's house, and folded fabric is in front of screen. Stool at center. Scenes 2 and 4: Screen, at right, covered with black cloth, represents cave in Andes Mountains. Downstage there is black cooking pot containing golden llama statue, and fire. (Fire may be made of wood and red cellophane with flashlight shining in center. A tin can of water with piece of dry ice in it may be placed behind pot to simulate smoke.)

Lighting: To heighten drama of earthquake scene, flash stage lights off and on, and/or shine large flashlight or spotlight, with red cellophane over lens, on Spirits.

Sound: Recorded South American flute music (or appropriate music), and rumbling sound of earthquake played on kettle or bass drum, as indicated in text.

The Deer Dance

About half of the population in the Central American country of Guatemala is Maya Indian, descendants of the great Mayan civilization that flourished in this area and in neighboring Yucatan between the 2nd and 10th centuries A.D. The Maya have retained much of their culture as it existed before the Spanish arrived in the early 1500s: They still speak dialects of Maya-Quiché, dress in traditional colorful clothes, and often practice old customs and rituals. This is especially true in the villages around Lake Atitlán, located in the highlands, which are above 5,000 feet. However, many Mayan people have adopted *Ladino* material culture, speak Spanish as a second language, and have blended their native religious elements with Catholicism.

The following dance drama is loosely based on the Deer Dance as done in Mayan villages around Lake Atitlán. This much-shortened version is aimed at giving a feeling for the dance and its characters. Traditionally, the Deer Dance involves elaborate and exacting preparations and prayers before the public presentation, which include several days of ceremonies and dancing; today it is rarely performed.

The Deer Dance

Characters

CAZADOR, (*hunter*), *an old man*
CATARINA, *his wife*
TWO PERRITOS, (*little dogs*)
TWO PASTORCITOS, (*shepherd boys*)
MOUNTAIN LIONS ⎤
JAGUARS   ⎟
MONKEYS   ⎬ *Animales, (animals)*
DEER   ⎦
MÚSICOS, (*musicians*)

TIME: *In the last century.*
SETTING: *Guatemala. Dark curtain backdrop. Candle and incense up left and down right.*
AT RISE: *Stage is empty. MÚSICOS (players of flute, maracas, chirimía, drum, and marimba) sit below stage. Flute player pipes a few plaintive notes, then starts a slow melody. CAZADOR, cane in right hand, maraca in left, enters right, hobbling, pausing, looking about, hobbling again, followed by CATARINA, carrying metal box, matches inside; she mimics his movements. They circle the stage, moving to music, ending center. All characters speak in chanting manner and move as if dancing.*

CAZADOR (*To audience*): I am the hunter, *El Cazador*, hunter of deer most of my life. Now I am old. Old and wise. *El Cazador* is a wise, old man. Into the forest still I hunt, into the hills I find the deer. I am *El Cazador*.

CATARINA (*To audience*): I am Catarina, the hunter's wife. I am his wife most of my life. Now I am old. Old and wise. Catarina is a wise, old wife.

CAZADOR: And we have *dos perritos*, two little dogs.

CATARINA: *Sí, dos perritos*, two little dogs.

CAZADOR: They help me hunt.

CATARINA: They make us laugh.

CAZADOR *and* CATARINA: We love our *dos perritos*. (*Flute ceases; maracas beat lively rhythm, punctuated by* CAZADOR's *maraca.* PERRITOS *enter right on all fours and to the amusement of* CAZADOR *and* CATARINA, *romp around, now and then pausing to pant, and ending up down left where, to the rhythm of maracas, they bark in union with different yelps, such as, "Woof, woof, arf, arf, bow, wow, wow," finishing with a long, loud howl.*)

CAZADOR (*To dogs*): Hush, *perritos*. (PERRITOS *freeze. Maracas cease. Flute music plays slow tune.*)

CATARINA (*To dogs*): Lie down. Go to sleep.

CAZADOR: Dream of hunting deer. (*Gently shakes maraca;* PERRITOS *whine and lie down on backs, feet in air.*)

CATARINA (*Smiling, scratches their stomachs*): Sleep, *perritos*, sleep. (PERRITOS *sigh with pleasure, curl up and sleep.*)

CAZADOR (*Pointing to dogs*): They will help me find the deer. Meat to eat and meat for *pesos*—that is how we live.

CATARINA (*Nodding*): That is how, that is how, that is how we live. (*Dances in hobbling manner with* CAZADOR. *When finished, they face audience. Flute music picks up tempo.*)

CAZADOR: And we have other helpers.

CATARINA (*Nodding*): Helpful helpers.

CAZADOR: *Dos pastorcitos*.

CATARINA: *Sí*, two shepherd boys. (*Flute ceases; chirimía plays a rollicking tune.* PASTORCITOS, *enter right and dance around in athletic manner, ending down right.*)

PASTORCITOS (*To audience*): We like to help *El Cazador* and Catarina. (*Flute plays along with chirimía as* PASTORCITOS *help* CAZADOR *and* CATARINA *dance forward.*)

CAZADOR: Soon we hunt the deer. Into the forest, into the hills. Soon we hunt the deer.

CATARINA: Careful, husband, careful. Danger hides inside the forest. Danger hides upon the hills. Danger all around.

PASTORCITOS (*Waving arms, in unison*): Danger hides inside the forest. Danger hides upon the hills. Danger all around.

CATARINA (*To* CAZADOR, *arms outstretched*): What would I do if I had not you? What would I do if you never came home?

CAZADOR: Do not worry, Catarina. With me go the little dogs, and with me go two shepherd boys. They will guard me if they can.

PASTORCITOS (*To* CAZADOR): We will guard you. (*To* CATARINA) We will guard him.

CATARINA (*Nodding to audience*): If they can, if they can.

CAZADOR (*Calling*): *Dueño* of the hills, protect us while we hunt.

CATARINA: Light the candle, light the incense. Honor the master of the hills. (CAZADOR *and* CATARINA *cross up left with* PASTORCITOS *and all kneel facing backdrop;* CATARINA *lights candle and incense.*)

ALL: *Dueño* of the hills, protect us (them) while we (they) hunt. (*Rise and cross to center*)

CAZADOR (*Calling to sky*): *Dueño* of the Window to the Sacred World, protect us while we hunt.

CATARINA: Light the candle, light the incense. Honor the master of the Window to the Sacred World. (CAZADOR *crosses down right with* PASTORCITOS *and they kneel, facing audience.* CATARINA *lights candle and incense.*)

ALL: *Dueño* of the Window to the Sacred World, protect us (them) while we (they) hunt. (*Rise and cross to center.* CAZADOR *shakes maraca and whistles loudly.*)

CAZADOR (*To dogs*): Wake up, *perritos*. Time to hunt the deer. (*Flute and chirimía cease and maracas play wildly as* PERRITOS *jump up and do a comical dance, tumbling, barking, leaping and racing about, occasionally pausing to pant.* CAZADOR *finally raises cane and shouts.*) Silence! (PERRITOS *freeze. Maracas cease. Flute plays.* CAZADOR *shakes maraca at dogs.*) Be serious now. You have a job. Listen! (PERRITOS *exchange looks, then cup ears.*) Will you help us hunt the deer? (PERRITOS *nod.*) Then, set your noses to the ground. (PERRITOS *put noses to ground. Pointing off left*) Now, go. Find the deer. (*Maracas play as* PERRITOS *run about, sniffling ground, then exit left. Maracas cease. Flute and chirimía play as* PASTORCITOS *and* CAZADOR *follow dogs. Chirimía ceases as* PASTORCITOS *exit.*) Goodbye, Catarina. Do not worry. Soon we bring home deer. (*He blows her a kiss, then exits.*)

CATARINA (*Waving, blowing a kiss*): Goodbye dear husband. Careful, careful. Danger everywhere. (*Flute plays a lonely tune as she crosses up left and blows out candle, setting it and incense in her box, then crosses down right and blows out candle, setting it and incense in her box. Blowing one more kiss over her shoulder toward left, she exits right. Flute ceases. Lights dim; green flood on. Deep drum beats in slow, mysterious fashion as* MOUNTAIN LIONS *and* JAGUARS *enter from left and right, creeping, crouching, slinking, glaring at audience, hissing, snarling, growling, a few stretching, a pair circling each other as if ready for a fight, then deciding against it. Finally, they exit as they entered. Drumbeat ceases. Flute, maracas, and chirimía play as* PERRITOS, *sniffing ground, and* CAZA-

DOR *and* PASTORCITOS, *with bows, cautiously enter left as if hunting.* CAZADOR *still hobbles but without cane and maraca. Sinister drumbeat added as a* JAGUAR *sneaks on left and a* MOUNTAIN LION *sneaks on right. They creep up and are about to pounce on* CAZADOR *when* PERRITOS *see them and bark a warning.* PAS-TORCITOS *pantomime shooting the* JAGUAR *and the* MOUNTAIN LION, *who snarl, leap in air and exit running. Sounds of quick, light drumbeats and maracas as* MONKEYS *enter, rushing in from all directions, whooping and chattering, scratching under arms, beating chests, picking off fleas, tumbling about.* PERRITOS *bark furiously at monkeys and chase them, but* MONKEYS *think it is a game and mock the dogs.* CAZADOR *and* PAS-TORCITOS *try unsuccessfully to chase monkeys away. Finally,* MONKEYS *exit as they entered. Drumbeat ceases.* PERRITOS, CAZADOR *and* PASTORCITOS *exit. Flute, maracas, and chirimía cease. Marimba plays.* DEER *gracefully leap on from right and left and dance about in ballet fashion. Maracas play and* PERRITOS *enter left sniffing ground; they see* DEER *and freeze, holding upstage hand in pointing manner, other hand extending tail.* DEER *freeze. At moment of freeze, marimba and maracas cease. Flute and chirimía play as* CAZADOR *and* PAS-TORCITOS *enter with bows, note dogs in pointing posture, then see* DEER. *All music plays in frantic manner as* PERRITOS, *barking, and* CAZADOR *and* PAS-TORCITOS, *pantomiming aiming arrows, chase* DEER *about stage. Finally,* DEER *exit in all directions.* PER-RITOS, CAZADOR *and* PASTORCITOS *chase one, exiting left. Music ceases. Lights up; green flood off. Flute music plays softly as* CATARINA *enters right, shades eyes with upstage hand and peers off left, sighs unhappily, then crosses to center.*)

CATARINA (*To audience*): My husband has hunted for many days. I miss him. I miss the little dogs and the shepherd boys. I miss them all. How lonely I feel! (*Sadly sinks to ground, hiding face in hands. Maracas and chirimía play along with the flute.* CATARINA *hears music, rises, peers off left, sees the returning party and claps her hands excitedly.*) I see them. I see them. The hunters are coming home. (PERRITOS *enter joyfully barking and circling* CATARINA, *who laughs and pets them, followed by* PASTORCITOS, *with deerskin cape, and* CAZADOR, *with cane and maraca.* CATARINA *hugs each of them,* CAZADOR *last.*)

CATARINA: Welcome home, my family. Welcome home.

CAZADOR (*Indicating off left*): We had much success, Catarina. The deer gave us meat. One gave you its cape.

PASTORCITOS (*Placing cape over her shoulders, in unison*): A deerskin cape for Catarina.

CATARINA: I thank you, and I thank the deer.

CAZADOR: And we thank the *Dueño* of the Hills.

PASTORCITOS: And the *Dueño* of the Window to the Sacred World.

CATARINA: *Sí.* They blessed your hunt.

CAZADOR (*Starts right, stretching arm back*): Come, my wife. (*Indicates* PASTORCITOS) Come brave *pastorcitos.*

CATARINA (*Smiling, indicating* PERRITOS): And our dear *perritos.*

CAZADOR: Come celebrate the deer hunt with feasting, with dancing, and with prayers. (*Music crescendos as* ALL *exit right. Curtain closes and music ceases.*)

THE END

Production Notes

The Deer Dance

Characters: Dancers with speaking roles—3 males, 1 female; dancers
without speaking roles—at least 10 males or females for animals;
musicians—5 male or female (might use older children or adults).

Playing Time: About 15–20 minutes, depending on amount of music
and dancing.

Costumes: Colorful Guatemalan peasant clothes, except for dogs, who
wear black or brown turtleneck shirts and matching tights with
yarn tails. All except musicians wear papier-mâché dance masks.
At times indicated in the script, the hunter uses a cane and carries
a maraca.

Properties: Small, lidded, tin box with matches inside, 2 candles, 2
incense cones, 3 bows, deerskin cape (cloth painted to look like
deerskin), musicians' instruments—flute, maracas, chirimía (an indigenous oboe—if not available, use a guitar), hand drum, marimba (if not available, use a xylophone).

Setting: Dark, backdrop curtain.

Lights: When indicated, dim lights and add green flood.

Additional Note: This dance drama is more successful when choreo-
graphed and the musicians follow the movements of their particular characters in a creative fusion of improvised melody and
rhythm that fits and enhances the type of characters, their moods,
and their actions.

The Sleeping Mountains

During the 15th and early 16th centuries, the Aztecs, a Nahuatl-speaking people, ruled a large empire in what is today called Mexico. They created a complex society, built huge stone temples, and amassed a great deal of gold. Then in 1519 Hernán Cortés, intent on establishing a colony for Spain, landed on Aztec shores with Spanish soldiers. Within a few years they had conquered the Aztecs, seized the gold, and instigated Spanish rule.

The legend of how Popocatepetl (Pô′ pô kä te′ pet⁹l) and Iztaccihuatl (ēs′ täk sē′ wät⁹l), two dormant volcanoes in south central Mexico, came to be is Aztec in origin, but the story of the twin sleeping mountains became part of Hispanic folklore, many versions still told today. Both volcanoes are snow-capped and over 17,000 feet high, among the highest peaks in the Americas.

The first recorded eruption of Popocatepetl was in 1347. It also erupted while the Spanish conquistadors looted the Aztec temples in the 1520s, leading the Aztecs to believe the gods were angry with what the Spaniards were doing. The name Popocatepetl means "smoking mountain" in Aztec, and from time to time the mountain still emits large clouds of smoke and occasionally spews forth clouds of ash and fiery rocks.

The Sleeping Mountains

Characters

KING PAPANTCO (*Pah-pahn'-ko*)
PRINCESS, *his daughter*
HIGH PRIEST
JAGUAR, *his son*
TWO GUARDS
KING IXTLI (*Eest'-lee*)
PRINCE, *his son*
SERVANT GIRL
TERANA, *attendant*
OLD WOMAN OF THE MOUNTAINS

SCENE 1

TIME: *A day when the world was young.*

SETTING: *The Courtyard of the Sun in the palace of King Papantco in the Valley of Mexico. There is a stone bench to the right of a well at center. To the left is a throne.*

AT RISE: SERVANT GIRL *is playing a gay tune on the flute.* GUARD *stands behind throne keeping time to the music by waving a large fan. In his belt is a sword.* TERANA *enters right, ushering* PRINCESS *to bench.* SERVANT GIRL *bows and exits left.* GUARD *stands at attention.*

PRINCESS: Where is my father, Terana?

TERANA (*Nervously*): The King and the High Priest have been holding a secret meeting all morning, my princess.

PRINCESS (*Shivering*): I do not trust the High Priest.

TERANA: Sh-h, Princess. It is not wise to speak against him.

PRINCESS: He holds too much influence over my father. And I do not like the High Priest's son, Jaguar! Every time I look at him, I am chilled all over. (*Sound of drum roll and horn blast is heard offstage.*)

GUARD (*Shouting*): To the Courtyard of the Sun comes King Papantco, the great Toltec ruler over all rich and green valley lands on the southern side of the mountains. (*GUARD and TERANA prostrate themselves. PRINCESS rises and bows.*)

PAPANTCO (*Entering right, followed by HIGH PRIEST*): A beautiful day! Rise, everyone. My daughter, you are as lovely as the feathers of the quetzal [*ket'-sahl*] bird. (*He sits on throne. PRINCESS sits on bench. GUARD waves fan over PAPANTCO, and TERANA stands behind bench.*) High Priest, bring your son, Jaguar, before me.

HIGH PRIEST: At once! (*Claps hands and makes magical gesture*) Itza! (*JAGUAR enters at once.*)

JAGUAR: Yes, Father!

PAPANTCO: Jaguar, we have been discussing you.

JAGUAR (*With a bow*): Oh, Magnificent King, I am honored that you would bring my name to your lips.

PAPANTCO (*To HIGH PRIEST*): He speaks well.

HIGH PRIEST: Of course.

PAPANTCO: His appearance is not the best I have seen.

HIGH PRIEST (*Quickly*): But, he is very loyal to you. I am teaching him many spells and potions. He will be a powerful friend for your empire.

PAPANTCO: Your words are convincing. (*Rises thoughtfully and crosses to PRINCESS*) Little flower, the time has come for you to be married.

PRINCESS (*Gasping*): To Jaguar?

PAPANTCO: The son of the most expert magician in my land would make an excellent husband for you.

PRINCESS (*Shocked*): Surely you would not wish me to marry one to whom I am so unsuited!

PAPANTCO: It is said that the mother corn will survive even on the desert. So you too can adjust. (*Crosses to sit on throne*)

PRINCESS (*Reaching for arm of* TERANA): But, Father—

PAPANTCO: Tomorrow your feathered wedding robe will be started. (*Sound of drum roll and horn blast is heard.* 2ND GUARD *enters.*)

2ND GUARD (*Shouting*): To the Courtyard of the Sun comes King Ixtli, the poor Chichimec [*Chee-chee-mek'*] ruler over all lean brown mountain lands to the north.

PAPANTCO (*Leaping up angrily*): Cactus spines!

2ND GUARD (*Continuing*): Accompanying King Ixtli is his son.

PAPANTCO: This is even more disgraceful. Two enemies in my palace.

HIGH PRIEST: By the tongue of the great feathered serpent, why are they here?

IXTLI (*Entering left, following by* PRINCE): I will be quick, for I find your land overrun with poisonous vines.

PAPANTCO: Since you prefer your rocky wasteland, I can see no reason for you to enter my fertile valley.

IXTLI: Your subjects are using my streams for fishing.

PAPANTCO: That is not true!

IXTLI: It *is* true!

PAPANTCO: You whine like a scrawny coyote.

IXTLI: My country is poor, but my people are proud. I will not take your insults.

PAPANTCO: Depart at once, or I will have you hung up on the tallest pyramid. (GUARDS *draw swords.*)

IXTLI: You would not dare. That would mean war.

PRINCE: Please, Father. You are pale. Let me handle this.

IXTLI: Handle it, then. I despise every moment I spend in this overgrown, foul-smelling land. (*Exits left*)

PAPANTCO (*Shouting after him*): Your land is full of prickly pears and rattlesnakes.

PRINCESS (*Crosses to him*): Please, Father. You are red. Let me handle this.

PAPANTCO: Gladly! (*Crosses right*) Guard, if the Chichimec Prince does the least thing to threaten the Princess, throw him into the well. (*Exits right, followed by* HIGH PRIEST *and* JAGUAR)

PRINCESS (*To* TERANA): Wait for me in the Room of Seven Paintings.

TERANA: But, it is not proper—

PRINCESS (*Gently waving her away*): Do not worry. I shall be careful. (TERANA *exits right.*) Guards, put your swords away and stand back. I do not need your protection immediately. (GUARDS *frown at* PRINCE, *and stand at rear.*)

PRINCE (*To* PRINCESS): I am sorry. It is not a pleasant way to meet.

PRINCESS: I understand. Our fathers have always been angry with each other.

PRINCE: Long ago they had a quarrel, and our two tribes fought. The reason for the quarrel is forgotten, but the bitterness remains.

PRINCESS: It is too bad. Our tribes should unite and be friends.

PRINCE: I am certain that if my people could see the lovely Toltec Princess, they would forgive anything. I know I do.

PRINCESS (*Blushing, looking away*): The Chichimec Prince is flattering, but he does not know me. (*Smiles shyly and indicates her robe*) You judge by my outward appearance.

PRINCE: A woman is only beautiful if she reflects goodness inside. I have met many women with perfect features whose faces became ugly with their thoughts. In your face I see kindness, gentleness, and honesty.

PRINCESS: I see goodness in yours. (*They stare at each other, then laugh in embarrassment, and look down.*)

PRINCE: Will you let me see you again? (JAGUAR *reenters stealthily, unseen by them, and hides behind well.*)

PRINCESS: I would like to see you very much, but my father has chosen Jaguar, a nobleman of my tribe, to be husband to me.

PRINCE: Do you care for him?

PRINCESS: No! I do not even like Jaguar.

PRINCE: Then, meet me in the forest tomorrow.

PRINCESS (*Crossing right, thinking, and crossing back to* PRINCE): If I should decide to meet you, where would it be?

PRINCE: Do you know the hut where the Old Woman of the Mountains lives?

PRINCESS: Yes. It is near the border which divides our kingdoms.

PRINCE: Meet me at the giant palm beside that hut.

TERANA (*Calling from off right*): Come, Princess, you take too much time.

PRINCESS (*Calling back to her*): I will be there. (*To* PRINCE) When the sun is rising. (*Loudly, to* GUARDS) Show the Chichimec Prince out of the palace.

PRINCE (*Bowing*): Princess, your courtesy is greatly appreciated. (*Exits left, followed by* GUARDS)

TERANA (*Reentering*): Ah, he has left.

PRINCESS (*Running to her*): I have much to tell you. First, you must promise to keep my secret.

TERANA: What is this? (PRINCESS *grabs her arm and pulls her right.*)

PRINCESS: Do you promise?

TERANA: Of course, but I am disturbed by this excitement of yours. (*They exit.*)

JAGUAR (*Coming out of hiding*): My pride is deeply stabbed. This enemy comes into our land and tries to steal that which belongs to me. So, the Princess does not wish to marry Jaguar! She will be sorry. (*Spits out words*) I shall make certain that evil overcomes them both. (*Curtain closes as JAGUAR exits right.*)

* * * * *

SCENE 2

TIME: *That evening.*

SETTING: *The Courtyard, the same as Scene 1.*

AT RISE: PRINCESS *and* TERANA *are sitting on the bench.*

TERANA: This is a terrible thing you are going to do.

PRINCESS: Why is it so terrible to meet someone?

TERANA: If your father knew, he would have the Prince killed.

PRINCESS: My father has little understanding of the heart of his daughter. (*Rises and starts to exit right*)

TERANA: My child, perhaps you will change your mind by morning.

PRINCESS (*Determinedly*): I will *not* change my mind. (*Runs back to sit by* TERANA) Come with me to the forest. It will give me more courage. I am not as brave as I wish I were.

TERANA (*Throwing up her hands in dismay*): Come with you. If I were caught, it would be the end of me.

PRINCESS: You are right. Forget what I have said. (*Rises*)

TERANA (*Rising*): Wait! I carried you on my back when you first visited the sacred well. I stayed beside you every moment you lay sick with the jungle fever. I will not let you go alone to the forest now.

PRINCESS: Thank you, dear Terana. I know I am asking much of you.

TERANA (*Patting her cheek*): Go to sleep now. I will awaken you before dawn. (PRINCESS *exits right.* TERANA *sighs and starts to exit left.* JAGUAR's *voice is heard from off right. She pauses.*)

JAGUAR (*From offstage*): The Princess meets the Chichimec Prince tonight. (TERANA *quickly crosses to hide behind well,* as HIGH PRIEST *and* JAGUAR *enter.*)

HIGH PRIEST: We must change our plans.

JAGUAR: You are right. She does not wish to marry me, and I believe she will find a way to change the King's mind. How can I become head of the kingdom now?

HIGH PRIEST: A bit of underhanded magic is necessary. (*Pauses*) If something should happen to detain the Princess tonight, then King Papantco would do anything to bring her back. (*Smiles maliciously*) It might be amusing to change the Princess and Prince into two stones for awhile.

JAGUAR: You run the risk of angering the gods.

HIGH PRIEST: Why should they care? The gods have never bothered me before. (*Pompously*) I think they are afraid of my powers.

JAGUAR: Perhaps you will become one of the gods, and people will worship you.

HIGH PRIEST: Perhaps! Come with me now. We shall mix a powder. You will take it to the meeting place and sprinkle it over the Princess and Prince. (*They exit left.*)

TERANA (*Running right, calling softly*): Princess! Princess! (*She exits. There is a moment's pause. She screams from offstage.*) Princess, where are you?

1ST GUARD (*Entering left, running, sword raised*): What is wrong?

TERANA (*Reentering, motioning for him to go away*): Nothing! Nothing! Return to your post. I had a bad dream.

PAPANTCO (*Entering right*): I heard a scream. What is wrong?

TERANA: It is nothing. I was dreaming—that is all.

PAPANTCO: But you are fully clothed. Guard, is the Princess safe? (*1ST GUARD starts to exit right. TERANA moves in front of him, blocking his way.*)

TERANA: She is fine. Do not disturb her sleep. Everything is well.

PAPANTCO: This woman is acting strangely. (*To 1ST GUARD*) See to the Princess. (*1ST GUARD exits. Nervously, TERANA begins to back away in the opposite direction.*)

1ST GUARD (*Shouting, from offstage*): The Princess is gone! (*TERANA turns and runs out.*)

PAPANTCO: Guard! (*1ST GUARD reenters.*) Bring back the attendant, Terana. (*He points offstage. GUARD runs off. Offstage, TERANA screams, then GUARD reenters dragging the struggling TERANA.*)

TERANA: Let me go! Let me go!

PAPANTCO: Where is the Princess?

TERANA: I cannot tell. (*Sinks to knees, sobbing*) I am sworn to secrecy. I promised the Princess I would not tell.

PAPANTCO: You dare refuse the request of your King?

TERANA: Oh, please, please, forgive me. The Princess is in danger. I must warn her. Let me go.

PAPANTCO: You will go nowhere until you tell me everything.

HIGH PRIEST (*Entering left, followed by JAGUAR*): What is the matter with the woman?

PAPANTCO: She tells me the Princess is in danger, but

she will not tell me where she is. (TERANA *rises and shrieks, pointing at* HIGH PRIEST.)

TERANA: He knows where the Princess is. Ask him!

HIGH PRIEST: The woman has lost her senses. I know nothing.

TERANA: You are evil. (*Whirls back to* PAPANTCO) All right. I will tell you where she is. She has gone to— (HIGH PRIEST *raises hands in a magic gesture, and* TERANA *gasps and sinks to floor.*)

PAPANTCO: She has fainted.

HIGH PRIEST: I will take care of her.

PAPANTCO: Guard, send a detachment of warriors to search the surrounding area. (1ST GUARD *exits left.*)

HIGH PRIEST: I suggest, King Papantco, that you try to rest. I am certain that by tomorrow this woman will give me the information we need.

PAPANTCO: This is most upsetting. (*Crosses right*) What could have happened to my daughter? (*Turns back*) If you find out anything, call me at once. (*Exits*)

HIGH PRIEST (*To* JAGUAR): Take this powder and go quickly. (*Gives pouch to* JAGUAR, *who holds it at arm's length*) Quickly! (JAGUAR *stealthily exits left, and* HIGH PRIEST *kneels beside* TERANA *as curtains slowly close.*)

* * * * *

SCENE 3

TIME: *Dawn.*

BEFORE RISE: PRINCE *enters left, before curtain, gazes right, and kneels to wait.* OLD WOMAN *enters right.*

PRINCE: Good morning, Old Woman of the Mountains. (*Rises*)

OLD WOMAN: Ah, Prince, what brings you to this side of the border?

PRINCE: The Toltec Princess.

OLD WOMAN: I can see by the radiance of your face that you would go anywhere to meet her.

PRINCE: You are right, Old Woman.

OLD WOMAN: It is dangerous. (*Shakes her head*)

PRINCE: I know. Our fathers are always on the verge of war.

OLD WOMAN: A pity! Lines are drawn, insults and spears are hurled. It is very difficult to love outside of one's tribe. (PRINCESS *enters right, sees* OLD WOMAN, *and stops.*) It is all right, Princess. I wish you both well. (*Exits left*)

PRINCE (*Crossing to* PRINCESS): I was afraid you would not come.

PRINCESS: There were times when my courage left me.

PRINCE (*Looking around*): You came alone?

PRINCESS: I did not wish to endanger anyone else's life.

PRINCE: You are braver than you realize. All night I have been awake, wondering what I should do. I want to ask for your hand in marriage.

PRINCESS: My father would never consent.

PRINCE: But, I cannot let you marry Jaguar.

PRINCESS: I will go with you to *your* father.

PRINCE (*Shaking his head*): My father would never accept you.

PRINCESS: Is there nothing we can do?

PRINCE: We could run away and leave both kingdoms. It would be difficult.

PRINCESS: If you will stay beside me, I am willing to go.

PRINCE: I will always stay beside you. (JAGUAR *sneaks in, and* PRINCE *sees him.*) Halt! Who are you? (PRINCESS *whirls around, gasps, and hides behind* PRINCE.)

PRINCESS: It is Jaguar!

PRINCE (*Drawing his sword*): Stand back.

JAGUAR: Your sword will be of no use to you, Chi-chimec Prince. (*Opens pouch and scatters powder over them.* PRINCE *and* PRINCESS *freeze, and* JAGUAR *laughs gleefully.*) I shall return for you, Princess. You will not *dare* refuse to marry me. Until our marriage takes place, the Prince will remain locked in his stone cage. (*Blackout*)

* * *

TIME: *Later that day.*
SETTING: *The Palace courtyard.*
AT RISE: KING PAPANTCO *is seated on his throne.* 1ST GUARD *stands behind him.* JAGUAR *sits on bench.* TERANA *kneels, bound and gagged, and* HIGH PRIEST *is speaking to the* KING.
HIGH PRIEST: Terana has revealed everything, King Papantco. The Princess has run away to marry the Chichimec Prince.
PAPANTCO: What? (*Rises; furiously*) We shall march against the Chichimec kingdom. (*Sound of drum roll and horn blast is heard.* 2ND GUARD *enters.*)
2ND GUARD (*Shouting*): To the Courtyard of the Sun comes King Ixtli, the poor Chichimec ruler over all—
PAPANTCO (*Interrupting*): He dares to return?
KING IXTLI (*Entering left; angrily*): Where is my son?
PAPANTCO: He kidnapped my daughter.
IXTLI: That is a lie. My son would not stoop to such a thing.
PAPANTCO: Stoop! Your son is a *cucaracha*.
IXTLI (*Sputtering*): I demand an apology!
PAPANTCO: Bah!
HIGH PRIEST (*Crossing between them and raising his arms*): Great kings of the northern and southern lands, I have a solution to this problem. My son, Jaguar, has courageously offered to find the Princess and Prince.

JAGUAR (*Rising*): King Papantco, I will bring your daughter back by nightfall, if you will consent to our marriage this evening.

PAPANTCO: What makes you so certain that you can bring her back?

JAGUAR: My father has given me special magical powers. And, if I should not succeed, you may sacrifice me to the gods! You see, I am most certain of my success.

PAPANTCO: Go, then! (*Sits on throne*) The wedding shall take place on your return.

IXTLI: What about my son?

JAGUAR: Later this evening he will be returned to your kingdom.

IXTLI: If he does not come back as you say, I promise to have every man in my kingdom armed with a club and on the march by morning.

SERVANT (*Entering right, excitedly*): There is a strange old woman here. The guards do not know how she managed to enter the palace.

PAPANTCO (*Rising*): Who is she? (OLD WOMAN *enters.*)

ALL (*In surprise; ad lib*): Who is it? How did she enter? (*Etc.*)

OLD WOMAN: Ah! Again the two enemy kings have met to snarl at each other.

IXTLI: Who are you?

OLD WOMAN: I am the Old Woman of the Mountains. Your son knows me well. I have lived long, longer than all of your lives together. (*Crosses to* HIGH PRIEST, *who backs away*)

HIGH PRIEST: Go away! You are not wanted here.

OLD WOMAN: Is that so, High Priest? Are you in charge of the world! Ah! (*Points at him*) Your magical powers have grown too large for your little mind.

HIGH PRIEST: How dare you speak to me in this manner! Away with you! (*Claps his hands and raises arms in magical gestures*) Itza! (OLD WOMAN *cackles, unaffected by magic.*)

OLD WOMAN (*In a loud, shrill voice*): The gods have grown angry with you, High Priest. You and your son have brought evil to this land. (*Moves toward them as they back up*) Like scavengers you sneak around and wait for the weak to fall. Henceforth, you are banished from the human race. You shall become animals, confined to the deserts and jungles, always hiding, always waiting, always living in the shadows.

HIGH PRIEST: No! No! (*Turns and runs off left, followed by JAGUAR. Loud howling and roaring of wild animals are heard from off left. All stare and move away from* OLD WOMAN, *watching as she unties* TERANA *and bids her rise.*)

PAPANTCO (*Cautiously stepping forward*): Old Woman of the Mountains, your powers are greater than ours. Bring my daughter back to me!

IXTLI (*Stepping forward*): Bring my son back to me!

OLD WOMAN: No! I do not choose to bring either of them back. They wish to be together.

PAPANTCO: But, the Princess must not marry the son of my enemy.

IXTLI: I cannot allow the Prince to marry my enemy's daughter.

OLD WOMAN: How silly you both are. (*Crosses to bench*) You are so wrapped up in bitterness that you do not really care about the dreams of your children. I have taken them to a place where they will always be together.

KINGS: What place?

OLD WOMAN (*Standing on bench and gesturing out over audience*): Look there. See those two beautiful mountains rising high above this valley? (*All stare in fear and wonder.*) Their names shall be Iztaccihuatl and Popocatepetl. The tops of the mountains are covered with a soft cloak of pure, white snow. Side by side these mountains will live while kingdoms below rise and fall. Some day, when there is less hate, the Princess and Prince will awaken and return to be happily married. Until then, they will sleep. And, when smoke rises from the mountains, it is to remind you that the Princess and Prince are indeed sleeping there. (KINGS *glower at each other and turn away, folding arms. TER-ANA weeps quietly, and SERVANT begins to play melancholy flute music, as OLD WOMAN looks about, shaking her head sadly, steps down, and slowly exits. Stage lights fade off as curtain slowly closes and music fades out.*)

THE END

Production Notes

THE SLEEPING MOUNTAINS

Characters: 7 male; 4 female.

Playing Time: 25 minutes.

Costumes: All wear simple costumes with an Aztec influence. Old Woman wears black. Prince and guards wear swords.

Properties: Pouch containing white powder, swords, large fan on the end of long stick, rope and handkerchief to bind and gag Terana, flute or recorder.

Setting: The courtyard of the Sun in the palace of the King Papantco in the Valley of Mexico. There is a well at center and a bench at right, both painted to look like stone. Throne is at left, painted gold, and draped with bright cloth. The backdrop is a painting of a dull red-colored plastered wall, with potted tropical plants hanging from it. Actual potted plants may be set upstage to give dimension to the backdrop.

Lighting: Scene 2 is a moonlit evening; Scene 3 is at dawn.

Sound: Horn blast (like a conch shell) and drum roll (played on a tom-tom); snarling wild cat, and howling coyote; flute or recorder music, played live, recorded, or whistled offstage by crew, if desired.

Macona, The Honest Warrior

The Carib Indians, once a fierce, warlike people, are most numerous in the dense rain forests of the Guianas (French Guiana, Guyana, Surinam) and in adjacent regions of Venezuela and Brazil from the Orinoco River south to the Amazon. The word "carib," from which the name of the Caribbean Sea is taken, originally meant cannibal, and was given to the Carib because they were known to raid hostile villages and to eat their prisoners. This was especially true of the Island Carib, who immigrated from the mainland to the Lesser Antilles. When Columbus came to the Caribbean in the late fifteenth century he was told terrifying tales of the Carib raids by the Indians of Haiti and Cuba.

Today the Carib are no longer cannibals, and they live deeper in the forests than when the Europeans first came. For the most part their lifestyle is the same as it was then, although some families have left to work on farms or in cities, and tourism plays a role in some villages. This play is based on one of the many stories told by the Carib, the same tales told before the arrival of Columbus in the Americas.

The tales of isolated indigenous peoples, such as the Carib, were never integrated into Hispanic folklore.

Macona, the Honest Warrior

Characters

MACONA
GREEN PARROT
RED PARROT
LUWANTAI
PRINCESS
OLD SORIBU, *her attendant*
CHIEF
TWO WARRIORS
MOSQUITOES, *extras*

SCENE 1

SETTING: *An Indian village in the Guianas, South America, near the Essequibo River. Upstage there is a Carib Indian house with working doorway. There is a fishing net lying on stage, beside steps. Aisle of auditorium represents river. There are two trees on opposite sides of stage steps. Several tropical plants are near backdrop.*

AT RISE: *Jungle animal sounds are heard from offstage.* GREEN PARROT *and* RED PARROT *are perched in trees, squawking, flapping wings, preening, and peering through leaves.* MACONA *is sitting on steps, mending the net.*

MACONA (*Disturbed*): For the second time this week my net has been broken and my fish stolen. (*Gestures and peers down audience aisle*) It must be a thief who moves silently along the Essequibo River. Is it an alligator? An angry spirit of the rain forest? Or could it be a warrior from the neighboring village (*Points*) up the river?

GREEN PARROT (*Flapping wings, squawking; in high voice*): It is not an alligator, Macona, for your net was cut with a machete.

RED PARROT (*Also flapping wings and squawking; in gravelly voice*): And there is not a spirit in the Guianas who would be angry with you, for your honesty and bravery are well known.

MACONA (*Rising*): Who speaks to me from the trees?

GREEN PARROT: I am Green Parrot.

RED PARROT: I am Red Parrot.

GREEN PARROT: We have magical powers.

RED PARROT: We speak when truth should be known.

MACONA: Do you know who stole my fish?

GREEN PARROT *and* RED PARROT (*Together*): We know. We know.

MACONA: How can I find out who it is?

GREEN PARROT: Leave your net in the river and hide close by. (MACONA *hides*.)

RED PARROT: Again the thief comes. See him pole his boat down the river. (MACONA *looks out from behind tree as* LUWANTAI, *wearing machete in waistband, enters at rear of auditorium and comes down center aisle. He pantomimes poling a pirogue—canoe—stealthily jumping ashore when he gets to steps.*)

LUWANTAI (*Seeing net*): There are some fine fish in this net. I will take them for myself. (*He pantomimes slashing net with machete, and then throwing fish into boat. He replaces machete in waistband and starts to shove boat into water.*)

MACONA (*Stepping out*): So, a warrior from our neighboring village is the thief.

LUWANTAI (*Angrily; pointing to himself*): How dare you accuse Luwantai?

MACONA: Tell me, Luwantai, are all your village warriors thieves, or is it just those too lazy to catch their own fish, like you?

LUWANTAI (*Shouting*): I am not lazy. (PARROTS *squawk as if laughing.*)

MACONA: If you are not a thief and you are not lazy, then how did my fish get into your pirogue?

LUWANTAI (*Nervously*): Well, ah, that is easy to explain. (*Sees* PARROTS, *who are squawking, and points to them*) The parrots in the tree did it. They threw the fish into my boat. (PARROTS *squawk loudly in protest.* LU-WANTAI *pantomimes pulling arrow from quiver, fitting it in bow, and aiming it at tree as he speaks.*) Those thieving birds will die by my poisoned arrows. (MACONA *pantomimes grabbing bow and arrow and hurling them into river.*)

MACONA (*As he does this*): I, Macona, will not let you kill these parrots.

LUWANTAI (*Angrily*): Not only do you falsely accuse me, Macona, but you steal my bow and arrow and throw them in the river. My village will hear about this.

MACONA (*Turning away, arms folded*): I am not afraid of you, Luwantai. You are a thief who uses boastful words. (*As* MACONA *speaks,* LUWANTAI *pantomimes shoving off pirogue, leaping into it, and then poling quickly down aisle to exit.*) I know who stole my fish, for I was hidden here and I saw you—(*Whirls to point, then sees* LUWANTAI *exiting, and calls defiantly after him*) This time you have escaped. But I shall come after you.

GREEN PARROT: Forget this thief, Macona. He will not return.

RED PARROT: It would be too dangerous to follow him to his village.

MACONA (*Pulling in net and throwing it off*): There is a code of honor among my people. A thief should pay with more than he takes. I must go to his village now and settle this matter. (*Pantomimes pushing pirogue off steps, jumping in, and then poling down aisle to exit*)

GREEN PARROT (*After* MACONA *exits*): There will be trouble for him.

RED PARROT: Surely the Chief of Luwantai's village will not harm Macona.

GREEN PARROT: Perhaps not. Perhaps he will. The minds of men work strangely.

RED PARROT: Let us fly to the neighboring village. Macona saved our lives. He may need our help. (PARROTS *come out of trees, flap wings as if flying; and exit; squawking. Curtain*)

* * * * *

SCENE 2

SETTING: *A neighboring village, where Luwantai's people live. House has been moved up center. One tree is at left and one is at right.*

AT RISE: PRINCESS *is sitting center, having her hair combed by* OLD SORIBU, *who kneels beside her. Sounds of jungle animals are heard.* MACONA *enters at rear of auditorium and comes down aisle, pantomiming poling pirogue to steps and beaching it.* PRINCESS *rises, startled, and* OLD SORIBU *stands in front of her protectively.*

MACONA: Do not be afraid. I will not harm you.

OLD SORIBU: I can tell by your headdress you come from the village down the river.

MACONA: Yes. I am called Macona. (SORIBU *and* PRINCESS *gasp and look around for others.*)

SORIBU (*Approaching him, whispering*): Leave at once,

Macona. Old Soribu warns you, for I wish no man harm.

PRINCESS (*Coming forward*): Go quickly. My father is the chief of this village. He has vowed revenge on you.

MACONA: Why?

PRINCESS: You insulted the warrior Luwantai.

MACONA: For good reason, lovely Princess. Luwantai is a lazy thief. Please believe me.

PRINCESS (*Turning sadly away*): It does not matter if I believe you. No one else in my village will. (*Turns to him*) Luwantai is my father's favorite warrior.

SORIBU (*Gesturing*): The Princess is promised to him in marriage.

MACONA (*Crossing to her*): It makes me sad that one whose hair shines more than a hummingbird's wings, whose eyes flash like fireflies in the dark, should marry such a man as Luwantai.

PRINCESS (*Smiling*): Though your actions are as bold as the jaguar, your words are softer than a butterfly. Please, Macona, go while there is time. (LUWANTAI *and* TWO WARRIORS *enter left, stealthily, unseen.*)

MACONA (*Kneeling*): No. Now that I have met the Princess, there is even more reason to expose Luwantai's deceit. (*Suddenly* LUWANTAI *and* WARRIORS *leap out from hiding, whooping loudly, and jump on* MACONA. PRINCESS *and* SORIBU *scream and move away, clutching each other.* MACONA *fights off* WARRIORS *and goes after* LUWANTAI, *who backs away fearfully.* WARRIORS *scramble to feet, and one grabs* MACONA's *arms while other holds his legs. They pull him back toward steps.*)

LUWANTAI: Tie him up. (WARRIORS *pantomime tying* MACONA's *hands and ankles.* LUWANTAI *crosses to house, calling*) Great Chief! I, Luwantai, your finest warrior, have captured the treacherous Macona. (*Crosses arms arrogantly*)

CHIEF (*From inside house; wildly, ad lib*): Ay ya ook! Ay kai ya! (*Etc. All stare at doorway. Suddenly* CHIEF *leaps out of house. He wears fierce-looking mask and raffia costume. He rushes about in circle, shaking costume. Finally he stops in front of house and leaps, with a yelp. Pointing to* MACONA) Macona, you shall die. (*With cry of anguish,* PRINCESS *rushes forward and kneels beside* CHIEF, *her arms raised pleadingly.*)

PRINCESS: No, no, Father. Please give Macona a chance to prove his innocence.

LUWANTAI: Do not listen to her, great Chief.

CHIEF: Rise, my child. Why do you interfere?

PRINCESS (*Rising*): Because I believe my father is fair enough to listen to both sides of any quarrel. (CHIEF *folds arms.*) Speak, Macona.

MACONA: Luwantai slashed my net and stole my fish. I saw him.

LUWANTAI: He lies. He lies.

MACONA: I speak the truth.

CHIEF: Hm-m-m. I believe Luwantai, but I will be fair. There will be a test. Whoever wins speaks the truth and marries my daughter.

LUWANTAI (*Startled*): A test? For me?

MACONA: Whatever the test, I will do it.

CHIEF: You must each go into the forest and carve a wooden stool before morning. On one side carve a monkey's head; on the other side—my face.

LUWANTAI: That's easy.

MACONA: I cannot do this, Chief, until I see your face.

CHIEF: You may not. I will not take off this mask all night, but still you must carve an exact likeness of me. (*To* PRINCESS) Princess, do not tell Macona what I look like, or you will be a traitor to our village. (*To men*) Remember, Macona and Luwantai, carve the stool by morning or you shall die.

PRINCESS: Father, this test is not fair. Luwantai knows what your face looks like.

CHIEF: Of course.

PRINCESS: How can Macona possibly know?

CHIEF (*Laughing*): He can't. (*To* WARRIORS) Cut Macona's bonds and let the trial begin. (*Exits into house. PRINCESS weeps on SORIBU's shoulder. WARRIORS pantomime cutting MACONA's bonds, then exit. MACONA thoughtfully rubs wrists. LUWANTAI crosses right, passing PRINCESS.*)

LUWANTAI (*Mockingly*): Poor Princess weeps for doomed Macona. What a pity! (*Exits right, laughing*)

PRINCESS (*Hurrying to* MACONA): Go back to your village. Save yourself.

MACONA (*With dignity*): I am a warrior, Princess. I will not run from danger. It is not honorable. (*Exits left. Lights dim to indicate passage of time. PRINCESS and SORIBU exit. Sounds of jungle animals are heard. PARROTS enter, climb into tree near steps. As lights go up half, LUWANTAI reenters, right, carrying block of wood. It has been partially carved.*)

LUWANTAI (*Yawning sleepily*): The night is only half over. There is plenty of time to finish carving my stool. First I will take a nap under this tree. (*Lies under tree at right and falls asleep. He remains onstage sleeping throughout following scene. Jungle animal sounds are heard. Lights go up three quarters. MACONA reenters, left, carrying block of wood and knife. He pantomimes carving.*)

MACONA (*Inspecting stool*): This stool is finished except for the Chief's face. What features should I carve? (*Looks at sky*) Soon it will be morning. (*Shakes head in despair*) It seems I have lost the Princess and my life.

GREEN *and* RED PARROTS (*Together*): Macona, Macona.

MACONA: Who calls?

GREEN PARROT (*High voice*): The magical parrots.

RED PARROT (*Gravelly voice*): You saved us from the poisoned arrows. Now we will save you.

MACONA: How can you help?

GREEN PARROT: The Chief sleeps in his house. (MACONA *looks at house and nods.*)

RED PARROT: We shall call our mosquito friends.

GREEN PARROT: They will enter his house—

RED PARROT: Crawl under his mask—

GREEN PARROT: And bite his face.

RED PARROT: Then he will throw off the mask—

GREEN PARROT: Run to the river—

RED PARROT: And splash cool water on his face.

MACONA: Then I shall see his face.

GREEN PARROT: Yes, yes, look closely.

RED PARROT: But don't let him see you. (MACONA *nods and hides behind tree, carrying stool.*)

GREEN PARROT (*Calling shrilly*): Gu yai ya, Mosquito, quick, quick, quick,.

RED PARROT: Gu yai ya, Mosquito, squaw-aw-ka-ka-ka-ka. (TWO MOSQUITOES *enter, buzzing, darting, and swaying, from right. They "fly" around stage, then enter house. There is silence. Then* CHIEF *yells and runs out of house without mask. He has two red circles on his cheeks and a star on his forehead. He leans over edge of stage and pantomimes washing face in river.* MACONA *peers out, touches his own cheeks and forehead, then smiles and nods. Meanwhile* MOSQUITOES *reenter from house and exit.* CHIEF *rises, looks about suspiciously.* MACONA *pulls his head out of sight.*)

CHIEF (*Muttering*) Pesky mosquitoes! (*Reenters house.* MACONA *comes out of hiding, pantomimes carving.*)

MACONA (*While carving*): Thank you, Parrots.

GREEN PARROT: We will stay close by.

RED PARROT: We will meet you again, Macona.

PARROTS (*Climbing from tree; together*): Soon, soon,

soon. (*They exit, squawking. Animal sounds are heard. Lights go up full.*)

MACONA (*Rising, looking at sky*): It is morning, and I am finished. (WARRIORS *enter, see* LUWANTAI *asleep and hurry over to him. They pick up the block of wood, shake heads in disgust and drop it, then awaken him.* LUWANTAI *jumps up nervously, hiding his block of wood.* PRINCESS *and* SORIBU *enter and stand sadly beside house.*)

CHIEF (*From inside house*): Ay ya ook! Ay kai ya! (*Etc. All stare at doorway. Suddenly,* CHIEF *leaps out, in mask, as before, and rushes around shaking raffia costume. Finally he stops in front of house and leaps with a yelp.*) Bring forth the stools. (MACONA *crosses to* CHIEF *and kneels, presenting stool.*) What is this? A likeness of my face. Amazing! Macona, how did you find out what I look like? (*Removes mask and gestures for him to rise*)

MACONA (*Rising, smiling*): To answer that question is not part of my test. (CHIEF *sets mask inside house.*)

CHIEF (*Smiling*): I meant to trick you. Instead, you have cleverly tricked me. Luwantai, where is your stool?

LUWANTAI (*Nervously*): Macona stole it.

CHIEF: What?

LUWANTAI: He stole it while I was ah—ah—resting.

1ST WARRIOR: Great Chief, Luwantai is not telling the truth. He slept all night.

2ND WARRIOR: His stool is hidden behind his back.

CHIEF (*Holding out hand*): Luwantai, give me your stool. (LUWANTAI *regretfully hands over block.*) So, this is how well you pass my trial. A block of wood scarcely carved. (*Holding stools side by side; sternly*) Which would you say is the better stool, Luwantai?

LUWANTAI (*Furiously, to* MACONA): This is all your fault. (*Whips out machete and rushes for* MACONA. *Just as his machete is raised high in air,* PARROTS *enter, "flying" and squawking loudly.*)

PARROTS (*Shrilly; together*): Stop! Stop! (LUWANTAI,

startled, turns to see PARROTS, *and* MACONA *grabs machete away.* LUWANTAI *snarls angrily, growls at everyone, and runs to exit. Those on stage move to backdrop and peer off after him.* LUWANTAI *shrieks in terror from offstage and reenters, pursued by angrily buzzing* MOS-QUITOES. *They fly about stage.* LUWANTAI *runs down steps and pantomimes pushing pirogue into river, leaping into it, and poling furiously up aisle, howling.* MOSQUI-TOES *follow. Meanwhile* CHIEF *places stools inside house, and* MACONA *puts machete into his waistband. All move forward to watch.* LUWANTAI *and* MOSQUITOES *exit.*)

GREEN PARROT (*Pointing wings to river; loudly*): A thief can never rest.

RED PARROT: Luwantai will be pursued forever.

CHIEF (*Extending hand to* MACONA): Macona (*Extends other hand to* PRINCESS) and the Princess will be married. May there always be friendship between our villages. (*All cheer as jungle animal sounds are heard and curtain closes.*)

THE END

Production Notes

MACONA, THE HONEST WARRIOR

Characters: 5 male; 2 female; 2 male or female for Green and Red Parrots; as many male or female extras as desired for Mosquitoes.

Playing Time: About 20 minutes.

Costumes: Carib Indians of the Guianas, South America. Chief wears fierce-looking papier-mâché mask head, with waist-length raffia attached as hair. Old Soribu wears gray wig or powdered hair. Macona and Luwantai wear feather headdresses and large earrings. Parrots wear their name colors in shirts and tights, and have cardboard beaks tied around heads. Mosquitoes wear black leotards. Parrots and mosquitoes have crepe paper streamers attached to arms for wings.

Properties: Torn fishing net (basketball net), machete (wooden or rubber toy), low, carved stool (papier-mâché) with monkey head on one side and face with red circles on cheeks and star on forehead on other side), and block of "wood," partially carved (use papier-mâché).

Setting: There is painting of rain forest of the Guianas on backdrop. Audience area represents Essequibo River, with aisle used as entrance. A cardboard cut-out of house, with working doorway, is upstage of steps, and fishing net is set up beside steps. Angled on opposite side of steps are two trees (stepladders covered with brown paper or burlap, with branches attached to audience side). Tropical plants are set near backdrop. In Scene 2, house is moved up center and one tree is moved to opposite side of stage.

Lighting: Lights dim and brighten as indicated in text, if such facilities are available.

Sound: Sounds of jungle animals, such as jaguar, monkey, frog, and macaw at times indicated in script, may be recorded or made by Mosquito actors.

Glossary

abogado—lawyer
abuela—grandmother
adiós—goodbye
alcalde—mayor
agua—water
¡Alto!—Stop!
amigo—friend
animales—animals
¡Ay!—Alas!
ayllu—ancient Inca village
bobo—foolish person
buenas tardes—good afternoon
buenos días—good morning
burrito—little burro, donkey
caballito—little horse
campesino—farmer, peasant
¡Caramba!—a common exclamation of surprise or displeasure
carreta—cart
castillo—castle
cazador—hunter
cerdos—pigs
chirimía—an oboe-like musical instrument
colones—kind of money in Costa Rica
condesa—countess
conejo—rabbit
coqui—small tree frog
cucaracha—cockroach
¡Cuidado!—Look out!
culebra—snake

de—of

de nada—you're welcome (colloquial); literally "it is nothing"

Dios—God

dos—two

dueño—owner, master

el—the (masculine form)

¡Escurite!—Scram!

faroles—transparent paper lanterns with lighted candles inside

fiesta—celebration, party, festival

fuego—fire

flamenco—a traditional type of Spanish dancing

frijoles—beans

gallinita—little hen

gallo—rooster

gato—cat

gracias—thank you

hacienda—an estate

hombre—man

hormiga—ant

juez—judge

la—the (feminine form)

Ladino—person of mixed Spanish and Indian blood (*mestizo*) or an Indian who has adopted Hispanic culture

las—the (feminine plural)

Latino—resident of the Americas of Spanish-speaking descent

llama—a woolly-haired, South American animal related to the camel

loco—crazy

los—the (masculine plural)

madre—mother

¡Madre Dios!—an exclamation; literally "Mother of God!"

mano—a stone used for grinding corn or grain

mantilla—a silk or lace scarf worn on the head over a high comb

maracas—gourd rattles

marimba—a musical instrument similar to a xylophone

médico—doctor

mestizo—person of mixed Indian and Spanish blood

mi—my

montaña—mountain

mucho—much, plenty

muchas gracias—thank you very much

músicos—musicians

muy—very much

nieve—snow

niño—child (*el niño* refers to the baby Jesus)

no hay posada—no shelter here

nube—cloud

olla—a clay pot or jar, usually used to hold liquids

padre—father

paella—pan-simmered chicken, rice, saffron, vegetables, shellfish

palo—small stick

papagayo—parrot

pastorcitos—shepherd boys

patio—courtyard

perritos—little dogs

perro—dog

peso—denomination of money used in some Hispanic countries

pícaro—rogue, scoundrel, rascal

piñata—paper-decorated form filled with candy and small gifts

policía—police

por favor—expression of politeness; please

posada—inn, shelter (*Las Posadas*—reenactment of Mary and Joseph searching for shelter) *pronto*—at once, right now

puna—high, cold plateau area in the Andes Mountains

¡Qué sorpresa!—What a surprise!

quipu—Inca recording device, using knotted, colored strings

ratón—small mouse

reales—former coins of Spain and Spanish America

reboza—a long scarf worn by women over the head and shoulders

saffron—yellow food flavoring from stigmas of a kind of crocus

sapo—large toad

señor—Mr., sir, gentleman

señora—Mrs., woman, usually married

señorita—Miss, young lady, usually unmarried

serape—blanket-like shawl or wrap, often worn over one shoulder

serpiente cascabel—rattlesnake

sí—yes

siesta—afternoon nap

sol—sun

sombrero—a broad-brimmed hat, usually with a tall crown

tamales—mixture of ground corn filled with cooked minced meat, then wrapped in a corn husk and steamed

tigre—tiger

tortilla—a thin pancake, traditionally made of corn

vamos—we go

viento—wind

y—and